MAKE IT TO
MIDNIGHT

Learning to Live When you want to Die

JIM DENNING

ISBN 978-1-64258-223-9 (paperback)
ISBN 978-1-64258-224-6 (digital)

Christian Faith Publishing, Inc.
832 Park Avenue
Meadville, PA 16335
www.christianfaithpublishing.com

Printed in the United States of America

INTRODUCTION

"The meaning of life is to find your gift. The
purpose of life is to give it away."
—Pablo Picasso

IT IS TEN o'clock on a normal Thursday evening in Texas in late 2014. A middle-aged man is sitting on the edge of his bed, contemplating his past and his future. He's petting his dog with one hand and holding a .357 Magnum in the other. His dog is lying next to him; sensing something is not right, the dog is lying a little closer than usual. The man replays the events in his life that have led him to the point of sitting in a darkened room; the only reason he doesn't put that .357 in his mouth and pull the trigger is his concern over who will take care of his dog. This evening was the culmination of years of anxiety, depression taking its toll. For years, he tried to pretend that he was fine; he would go to work, put on the happy face, and muscle through it; but one day, he finally broke.

The debate whether to end his life or not may seem absurd to the casual observer. This man has a great job, great friends, and a great life, from all appearances. He was living the dream; he had a fantastic job travelling the country as an IT engineer, spending weeks in wonderful places and seeing all the local sites . . . all on someone else's tab. His life was pretty close to perfect, yet he struggled just to make it through the day; all he could think about was how he could not take the emotional pain anymore. He looked at the rest of his life and saw nothing worth looking forward to; he felt nothing but sadness and hopelessness awaiting him.

On the rare occasion that he would confide in someone about how he was feeling, they were always shocked to hear he struggled with depression and anxiety. Upon telling them about his struggles, he would hear things like "Seriously? You're always in such a good mood" or "What in the world do you have to be depressed about?" These responses only served to reinforce that he was doing an excellent job of acting and hiding what he was really feeling, but they also cemented the feeling that he was weak. When he heard "What do you have to be depressed about?" he never had a good answer; the only answer that was logical was that he was not strong enough to live life so he should not try anymore. This was an incredibly dark place.

As he sat on the bed staring at the gun, the minutes ticking by, he started recalling his life and what he had done. He remembered the fun he had in college, the great times with his friends, the fantastic parties they had thrown, and the countless nights they had spent watching bad television shows. He recounted the wonderful experiences he had as a consultant, travelling across the country and the great vacations he had gone on. While he remembered all these events, he felt no joy in them; the depression had not only robbed him of his present happiness, but his fond memories as well. He had reached the point where joy was no longer attainable and all that was left was emptiness and hopelessness. Depression had robbed him of his past and anxiety had stolen his future.

While he was sitting there in the dark trying to find a reason to put the gun back in the drawer, he remembered the time when he was a volunteer doing ministry work in a prison. He remembered one evening he was leading a Bible study, and after the study had ended, he was talking with a man named Mike. Mike was a tall, thin man from Louisiana who had been incarcerated on drug charges. He recalled a conversation with Mike from years before when had asked Mike what he planned to do when he got out, how was he going to stay sober living in the outside world. Mike thought about it for a minute and smiled at him and said in a thick Cajun accent, "Jim, I'll be honest with you, one day is as big a bite from life as I can take. I have no idea what I'm going to do when I get out of here. I couldn't tell you what I'm going to do tomorrow. I don't know what I'm gonna be doin' this week or next week because I can't promise I'll make it to next week. I can only promise this: I'll make it to midnight."

The man with the gun was me, and that day was just a few years ago. I didn't realize it at the time but what Mike so casually said to me would forever change my life. It was at this time that I was at my lowest point and that little phrase "I don't know what I'm going to do tomorrow. I can only promise you this: I'll make it to midnight" saved my life. That night, at 10:30 PM, I put down the gun, took my dog for a walk, and made it to midnight. I had taken my first step toward a new life.

My journey into the abyss started on December 4, 2009 at 2:00 PM—that day something in my brain snapped. I really cannot fully explain what it was, but it felt like something in my mind had reached the breaking point and it finally collapsed. The best way I can describe it is that the years of pressure from day-to-day life had finally broken the last timber that was holding my mind together. Over the course of that year, some things had happened that had a pronounced effect on me, and my best guess is that those events, coupled with things that happened when I was younger that I had not resolved, resulted in the events of that day. I vividly remember sitting at my desk, at what I considered to be a very cushy job, and this overwhelming urge to burst into tears washed over me. It was like a wave of utter hopelessness had washed across me and my brain could no longer hold it back, so I didn't. I quietly went down to my car and sat in the driver's seat and bawled like a baby, and to this day, I have no idea why. I know what lead to that day, but I do not know why I snapped so suddenly and violently. The next few months were hell. I didn't know how deep despair could go.

Over the course of the next six years, I fought with all the means at my disposal against the depression and anxiety and the desire to end it all. I initially sought the help of medical professionals, then mental health professionals. After that, I leaned upon the experiences of others either in person or on web forums. When I reached the point that I realized that I was not improving with outside assistance,

I decided to pursue a degree in counseling. This may sound extreme, but what I could not get my head around was why a person like me, who had so much going for, was so incredibly, hopelessly depressed. There had to be answers, and it seemed a university was the best place to find them.

What I did not realize at the time was that all these resources that I was tapping into were providing me valuable information; however, it took me considerable time to realize that these seemingly disjointed resources were, in fact, giving me all the tools I needed to overcome my condition. God had given me all the tools and resources to crawl out of this hole I was in; it just took me time to sort through the toolbox and use the tools in a proper fashion. For example, if I was going to build a house, I had to first lay the foundation, then I could acquire the lumber. It is only after the lumber had been measured and cut that I could assemble the framework for the house. Finally, once the frame of the house was assembled, I could add the roof and sheetrock the walls. In my journey, I discovered the same thing; not all the resources that I marshaled to help me were useful, but most were. Some of the things I tried had to be cast aside and some ended up in the toolbox. Even when I did come across a useful tool or resource, I had to put them in the right order and then learn how to use them. My hope is that with this book, I can save you the trouble of repeating the trial-and-error process I went through.

This book is meant to be something that hopefully contains information that other people can add to their toolbox to help them deal with, and eventually overcome anxiety and depression, and if they do reach the point of being suicidal, like I did, they can see that there is a beautiful light at the end of the tunnel they are living in. The best thing about emerging from that tunnel is that after you emerge from a season of darkness, the light is twice as bright and it is beautiful. I have successfully emerged from that tunnel; I went from sitting on the edge of my bed struggling to find a reason not to end my life to sitting on top of the world, and all of it without medication. If you are walking in the valley of the shadow of death, please remember: if you can just "make it to midnight," that light is one day closer.

CHAPTER 1

Diary of a Madman

"A hero is one who knows how to hang on
one minute longer."
—Novalis

FOR YEARS, I struggled with depression and anxiety, and after a long period of time with no relief from traditional sources, my depression and anxiety drove me to the point that I wanted to end my life. For several years, I struggled with something called suicidal ideation. Suicidal ideation is the fancy term for being so depressed or anxious that you lose hope, and this loss of hope manifests itself in the desire to take your own life. I intentionally use the phrase "I struggled with suicidal ideation" and not that I *am* or *was* suicidal, primarily because being suicidal is a label and a definition of me as a person; that is definitely not the case. I am a person who struggled with suicidal ideation, but now I have been freed from that struggle. This may seem like simple semantics on its surface, but it is a very important distinction. For example, if a person is overweight, they may say to themselves, "I am fat." In saying "I am fat," they are defining themselves as fat and not as a person. They are not fat; they are a *person* who struggles with maintaining their desired weight. If they see themselves as a person who struggles with maintaining their weight, they can also see a day where they are at their desired weight.

By separating the person from the struggle they are experiencing, it is much easier to see a future where that challenge has been overcome.

When I was in the depths of my depression, I began saying "I am depressed." That was a true statement, but when I started to define my depression as a component of my psyche and not the totality of my situation, I was able to isolate it as a problem that could be and was defeated. If one day you're driving down the road and your check engine light comes on, you realize something is wrong with your car. You take it to the auto shop and they hook it up to a machine and it tells you the alternator has gone bad. Upon hearing this news, you don't say "My car is broken" and just accept it as fact and leave your car to rot, or in my case, the metaphor would be destroying the car because one part is faulty. In this scenario, you identified the problem as the alternator; you have the alternator replaced and you drive away. Obviously, depression and anxiety are far more complicated than replacing an alternator, but when I started seeing my depression and anxiety separate from me, as a person, I began my road to recovery.

I will always struggle with depression and anxiety for the rest of my life; that's just how I am built. My brain was put together in such a way that I will have to mitigate that part of my personality and take appropriate steps to not let it dominate my day. We will discuss this later in the toolkit section. Depression and anxiety may rob me of a day, but they will not rob me of my life. That is what *Make it to Midnight* is all about. My struggle may get a few hours or even a day from me, it may get a series of days, but it will *not* take my life. Depression and anxiety are symptoms of a problem. In themselves, they are not the problem, just like a dead battery is a symptom of a bad alternator, not a bad car. Understanding what the real structural problems were was my first step to correctly diagnosing what was causing me to feel the way I did.

The circumstances behind my condition are relatively unimportant. While many people end up at the crossroads of deciding whether to continue their journey of life or take the next off-ramp and end it (if we experience suicidal ideation), we all end up at this intersection in our lives by different routes. Some got here just by an accident of genetics whereas some experienced trauma along the way that has made them question whether life is worth continuing or not. I think debating the circumstances that brought us to this point in our lives will turn this discussion into a comparison of stories, and by extension, an old-fashioned pissing contest that will diminish the fact that we are all facing the same decision: do I let the game end or keep pumping in quarters hoping to get to the next level?

I spent a lot of time trying to find a way to figure out why I felt the way I did. Why was I so hopelessly depressed? Why was I so anxious about my future? Then one day, I realized something: I was an addict without a drug. Many addicts use their addiction as an escape from reality; they use it as a coping mechanism for their problems. When alcoholics have a bad day, they drink. Those addicted to stronger drugs do the same thing. As an addiction counselor, I saw this over and over when a client relapsed. Now, do not get me wrong, I am not in any way blaming or disparaging the addict because addiction is a horrible situation to be in. The reason I was not an addict is that I had not tried enough drugs to become one. I have no doubt had I tried heroin or cocaine or any of a myriad of other options I would have become an addict like Mike, and my *Make it to Midnight* story would be one of addiction and not suicidal ideation. What I realized about addicts is that the pain of life had become greater than the fear of the consequences of acting out their addiction, so they would relapse. My problem is that I do not have the luxury of a relapse . . . or even a lapse! If I decided to act out, it would happen one time.

At the depth of my depression, I pondered becoming an alcoholic, or even trying heroin. My irrational mind had told me that I was going to be this way forever and I might as well enjoy the ride as much as possible. There was even one time when I was convinced that my dog was the problem, and if I had no responsibilities, I could be free . . . so I should put Tahoe down. I cannot believe it got that bad. Fortunately, my love for Tahoe is greater than that. One crazy idea I came up with was to commit a felony so I could go to prison! I'm serious! The logic was that I would be able to rest in prison. I had to remind myself that I was not prison material, and having volunteered in prison for as long as I did, I would be in much worse shape than I am now. Again, the one thing that kept me going was my mantra, just "make it to midnight."

Anyone observing me would have to come to the conclusion that I had a great life, and to be honest, I did a great job of portraying that façade to everyone I knew—well, almost everyone. I had let very few friends in on my secret. People I have spoken to about this have often asked me, "Why did you want to kill yourself?" It is difficult to explain to people how suicidal ideation works. Suicidal ideation is as if a switch has been flipped and the grim reaper is always waiting in the wings for a bad day when he can tap you on the shoulder and quietly say, "You know you do not have to endure this . . . one bullet can make all this go away." I never wanted to kill myself; I just wanted the pain to end. I would be at work, sitting there in the midst of a full-blown panic attack, struggling with all my strength to put on the façade of having a good day and this calm and quiet voice in my head would say something like "Jim, you don't have to do this. You know you have a gun at home, you could just get up from your desk right now and walk out of the office, drive home, grab the gun and in an instant this would all be over." I'll be honest, that is a very seductive thought in the midst of a dark time. There is a part of me that thought the voice was demonic, but I hesitated to follow that line of reasoning simply because if I blamed a demon, the problem would be out of my control. I needed to keep this problem in-house; otherwise, I would be powerless to fix it. The voice was not loud or overbearing; it was a very calm and soothing voice. It would say, "Just a simple pull of the trigger, and all the pain will be gone." The problem is the pain would not be gone. All I would be doing would be taking my pain and thrusting it upon someone else . . . everyone else. If I had ended my life, I would leave many people behind who would, for the rest of their lives, ask themselves, "What could I have done?" Promise me and yourself this: before you decide to end your life, just pick one person who would miss you and tell them your plan. Don't do it for you . . . do it for them. If they are your friend or family, do not rob them of the blessing of helping you. Do not sentence them to a life of wondering what *they* did not do that they could have done to help you "make it to midnight."

I vividly remember one morning driving to work listening to an audio Bible, and Job chapter 10 started playing and I completely saw myself in Job that morning. I think anyone who has experienced deep depression can relate to what Job was going through:

> *I loathe my very life; therefore, I will give free rein to my complaint and speak out in the bitterness of my soul. I say to God: Do not declare me guilty, but tell me what charges you have against me. Does it please you to oppress me, to spurn the work of your hands, while you smile on the plans of the wicked? Do you have eyes of flesh? Do you see as a mortal sees? Are your days like those of a mortal or your years like those of a strong man, that you must search out my faults and probe after my sin—though you know that I am not guilty and that no one can rescue me from your hand? "Your hands shaped me and made me. Will you now turn and destroy me? Remember that you molded me like clay. Will you now turn me to dust again? Did you not pour me out like milk and curdle me like cheese, clothe me with skin and flesh and knit me together with bones and sinews? You gave me life and showed me kindness, and in your providence watched over my spirit. "But this is what you concealed in your heart, and I know that this was in your mind: If I sinned, you would be watching me and would not let my offense go unpunished. If I am guilty—woe to me! Even if I am innocent, I cannot lift my head, for I am full of shame and drowned in my affliction. If I hold my head high, you stalk me like a lion and again display your awesome power against me. You bring new witnesses against me and increase your anger toward me; your forces come against me wave upon wave.*

"Why then did you bring me out of the womb? I wish I had died before any eye saw me. If only I had never come into being, or had been carried straight from the womb to the grave! Are not my few days almost over? Turn away from me so I can have a moment's joy before I go to the place of no return, to the land of gloom and utter darkness, to the land of deepest night, of utter darkness and disorder, where even the light is like darkness. (Job 10:1–22)

I completely felt what Job was feeling. I felt as if God had abandoned me and there really was no hope. I felt that I was being punished, but I had no idea what for and the voice was there to tell me it was all my fault. That voice was very insidious for me, because it was quiet and calm, and unfortunately, it made some pretty convincing arguments. I decided to call this voice Slick. I pictured him as me, except he wore a black suit with a red shirt and a thin black tie. I pictured him as the evil side of me. Again, I did not picture Slick as a demon. Although the definition would have fit; Slick felt like part of me, not something outside of myself.

Every pilot and most people know the phrase "point of no return." It is the point in a flight where you must proceed to your destination because the airplane has proceeded to the point that there is not enough fuel to return home. This is true of life as well; the decisions we make on the first half of our journey will dictate the second half; there will come a point where we have crossed the midway point in our journey and will no longer be able to turn around if the trip did not go as planned. This is where I found myself. I was looking at every life decision I had made up to this point and while I believed they were the correct decisions at the time, unfortunately, Slick was working overtime trying to convince me otherwise. The Germans have a word for this phenomena, which is *torschlusspanik*. Loosely translated that word means "gate-closing panic," but its contextual meaning refers to "the fear of diminishing opportunities as one ages."

In this dark place, all I could think about were decisions in my past that I had made and how they were all wrong. "Why didn't I do this?" "Why did I do that?" It's almost as if Slick was living in my head, playing back every negative thing that happened in the most negative light possible. Everything I have no control over somehow became my fault. My dad had a nugget of "dad wisdom" he would share every so often when I would regret something. It was "No sadder words from tongue or pen than those sad words 'what might have been.'" And while I know this to be true, Slick was always there to remind me of every fork in the road I have taken in my life and then pick them apart; he was tireless and relentless. Every relationship that ended, regardless of the circumstances, every job I have left is prominently displayed on the jumbotron of my mind. Then immediately after I see the moment I left that job or relationship, I am shown an alternative ending to what my life would have been like had I not left that relationship or changed jobs. The vision that was displayed on the screen was of me living happily ever after with a great job and wife and dog . . . If I had only taken the other fork in the road, but now it's too late. All the replays have one common theme, which is, "Jim, you caused your pain and it was avoidable, but you're too old to change it now so you should just end it." The obvious conclusion of these replays is that I had a chance for happiness and a peaceful life, but I blew it. Then Slick would go for the knockout with something like "You know, you are middle-aged now. It's too late to start over. Why don't you just end it? Come on, I'll help you load the gun."

Slick was not only good at pointing out my mistakes in the past, but he had a penchant for stealing positive memories as well. Something I learned about deep depression is that while I was unable to experience joy in things I was doing in the present, I was also unable to experience the joy in things I had done in the past. I have taken numerous wonderful vacations, and like everyone, I would think back to those times and be able to relive the happiness from those trips, but as the depression deepened, my ability to feel joy from past events went away. I could remember the trips and the fun we had on a cognitive level, but I could not *feel* the joy.

Slick was also a biblical scholar. Okay, I have a master's degree in ministry. I'm a biblical scholar, and he lives in my head, so technically, we are both biblical scholars. Slick wanted me to break so badly that he started pointing out scriptures. When Slick was trying to convince me to end it all, he would bring up scriptures like Matthew 11:28–30

> *"Come to me, all you who are weary and burdened, and I will give you rest. Take my yoke upon you and learn from me, for I am gentle and humble in heart, and you will find rest for your souls. For my yoke is easy and my burden is light."*

While Jesus meant for us to come to Him in this life, Slick was able to twist Jesus's words to be an invitation to end my life and go join Him in Heaven now. I remember several years ago, in the midst of my darkest time, I attended a funeral for a friend of mine who had died in an accident. I was somber like all others in attendance and was saddened that a life had been cut short. Then I began to read the program. At the bottom of the program was a closing that read, "Now, my son, you can rest." I remember crying when I read this, not because I was saddened for the loss of a friend, but because I was jealous. I was jealous that his pain had ended and mine had not. I am ashamed to admit that this is how I felt, but for the persons who are struggling with suicidal ideation, they will understand.

After the funeral, I realized that it was time for Slick and me to have a talk. The first thing that I did was to block out some time where I could be alone. I grabbed a beer, a cigar, and my dog and had a long conversation with myself. I told Slick that regardless of what he said or how much he pestered me, I was not going to eat a bullet for him. I explained that he could talk all he wanted, but it wasn't going to happen. I told him, in no uncertain terms, that the last conversation my friends and family have about me will *not* be that I killed myself. I will not be the one who chisels the end date of my life onto my own tombstone. I absolutely refuse to be remembered that way. My suicide was not a leaf I was going to hang on the family tree.

One thing I learned from this ordeal is that how you talk to yourself makes a tremendous difference. We will cover the science of that in later chapters, but from the beginning of this book, I want you to start paying attention to how you talk to yourself. Learning to talk to yourself in a complimentary and noncritical fashion is one of the most important survival skills you can learn. I learned that if I can "beat myself up," I can lift myself up too.

That night, I went on my back porch and sat down with my dog. I cleared my head, opened my beer and lit my cigar. While I was having my beer and cigar, I told Slick that we were roommates from here on out, and this was not a short-term lease. I literally had this conversation in my head; I said that we were in a bad spot, and we needed to work together to figure it out. I know this all sounds completely nuts, but just stick with me here; it will all make sense. I spoke to Slick as if he and I had been friends for years. I reminded him of all the good and bad times we had in our life and looked to him for answers of why we were in this situation. I asked him directly, "We have such a good life, why are you doing this to us? Why do you want us to die?" It was at this moment that something unexpected happened . . . I got an answer.

He told me his biggest concern was that someday I would lose my job because of the depression and anxiety, and we would starve to death on the streets. His concern over our well-being was ironically the cause of the anxiety and depression, as well as the result. He told me that he was so tired from stressing and working all the time to maintain our lifestyle, so he didn't want to go on, but that we couldn't quit working because we would lose everything; we would be homeless again. I broke down crying; it now made sense. Years ago, I had made a series of bad relationship decisions and ended up homeless. Slick's biggest fear was that it was going to happen again, and to be honest, on the trajectory we were on, it was a possibility. I had worked so hard to get ahead and make sure that didn't happen, that there was a part of me that just got burned out. That part was Slick, and he wanted to rest, and since I refused to let him, he wanted to die.

For years, he had been trying to tell me in a subtle way to quit pushing so hard, quit going to school, quit working crazy hours, quit traveling, and just relax; but I didn't listen. He kept talking louder and louder, and I kept not listening. When he was screaming, I turned to medication and alcohol to silence him and kept pressing on. And finally, on December 4, 2009 at 2:00 PM, Slick quit asking. On that day, he decided the only way to get me to rest was for us to die and that was his mission. All this time I was so angry and frustrated with that voice in my head, and at the end of the day, it turns out I owed him an apology. So that's exactly what I did. We had hit rock bottom, and we hit hard. As we stood there at the lowest point of our lives, we looked up at what would prove to be a very long climb, but we were going to do it together.

By this point, we were so burned out, mentally and emotionally, that our task seemed almost impossible; we had decided that we were going to live, but we had not discussed why. We had no hope, no plan, and no strength. It was then I remembered something that one of the female inmates told me when I was volunteering in the prison. She was a lady, around thirty years old; you could tell she had lived through some seriously hard times, but she still had an amazing dignity about her. She had lost everything that meant anything to her. She had lost her home, her children, and her family had turned their backs on her. One night we were in our group and people were discussing their faith and how it helped them cope with prison. She said something I will never forget; she said, "I didn't know God was all I needed until God was all I had." I had heard similar things before in church, but I had never heard them from someone who truly lived it. Those were powerful words, powerful enough for Slick and me to realize that we didn't have a reason to live, but God had a reason for us to stick around.

CHAPTER 2

The Conflict Within

"The greatest conflicts are not between two people
but between one person and himself."
—Garth Brooks

FREUD WAS THE first mental health professional to come up with
the idea of multiple components to our psychic apparatus; he called
them the id, ego, and superego. However, Paul, in the Bible, was
the first one, that I am aware of, to present the idea; he wrote in
Galatians 5:17:

> *"For the flesh desires what is contrary to the Spirit,
> and the Spirit what is contrary to the flesh. They are
> in conflict with each other, so that you are not to do
> whatever you want."*

We will give Paul credit for the concept and Freud credit for
coming up with the names. According to Freud, the id is our instinc-
tual primal self that is only interested in seeking pleasure and avoid-
ing pain. Conversely, the superego is the part of our psyche that helps
us determine right from wrong. However, what Freud did was give
a scientific name to something that the Bible identified millennia
before. Christians call those components of our psyche the flesh and
the spirit. The flesh, which is the Christian equivalent to the id, is

the part of us that is primal and self-serving. The flesh has no concept of past or future; it only is concerned with the now and getting the current needs met, no matter the cost to anyone else. It is fascinating how close to Freud that Paul is in his statement. "They are in conflict with each other, so that you are not to do whatever you want." Well, that conflict that Paul refers to is what Freud aptly named the ego.

The flesh lives in the moment and is profoundly selfish. Newborn babies, for example, are purely id, purely flesh. If it is three o'clock in the morning and the baby is hungry, it will scream and cry until someone arrives to satisfy its hunger. The baby only knows that it is hungry and crying brings people who make the hunger stop. It is important not to misinterpret how the flesh sees things. The flesh is not really "selfish" as being selfish is a decision that presupposes knowledge that someone other than the self exists. A baby crying in the middle of the night is not really being selfish, as the baby has no concept that it is a person and that other people are being inconvenienced by the late-night interruption. The baby is not making a decision to wake someone up out of disrespect or a feeling of entitlement, the baby only knows its own needs. This will be important when we contrast the flesh with the other parts of the psyche.

Conversely, the part of the brain that Freud called the superego is what Christians call "the Spirit." The spirit is our moral compass. As we grow from childhood into adulthood, our spirit becomes stronger as the executive parts of our brain grow. While the spirit may be seen as something ethereal, I believe that it is actually a part of our brain designed by God to allow us to consciously do His will. The spirit is the component of our brains that uses the word "should." I *should* not rob a bank even though I need money. I *should* not cheat on a test even though I didn't study. I *should* not smoke cigarettes because they are bad for me. The spirit is the part of our brain that weighs the consequences of our actions and helps us to determine whether or not to take that course of action. The spirit is the logical part of our brain. It has a database of the laws it is aware of, the experiences of its past, and the lessons learned from others. This is the part of our brain that learns the rules and laws that govern us and evaluates our actions and intended actions against them. This is the part of your brain that reads the calories on the pack of doughnuts and the alcohol content on a bottle of beer and then tells the flesh that we are not going to have doughnuts and beer breakfast because being drunk and fat is no way to go to work.

Every person starts out as purely flesh, but as they get older and as their brain develops, assuming no trauma or genetic abnormality, they will begin to develop a sense of what is right and what is wrong. They begin to develop consciousness or, as the Bible calls it, "the spirit" and Freud named it the superego. When the baby grows into a child, the child will begin to learn to make decisions based upon the needs of the flesh, but those needs will be evaluated through the filter of how the means to support those needs impacts the larger community. For example, if the child wakes up at three o'clock in the morning and is hungry, the child may have the desire to yell for his or her parent, but that decision, whether to yell or not, will be tempered with the knowledge that the parent has to wake up in the morning for work. That decision will also be measured against what a child of his or her age "should" be able to do. "Should" a five-year-old be yelling for a parent when he or she is hungry in the middle of the night? "Should" a child of that age be able to walk into the kitchen and pour a glass of milk and find a cookie? Has the child been given permission to eat the cookies? If not, who wins the struggle between the spirit and the flesh? Does the spirit win? The spirit, who knows eating the cookie is wrong, or does the flesh win? The flesh, who really wants the cookie, is unconcerned with the consequences because it only cares about two things: what the flesh wants (the cookie) and when the flesh wants it (which is now). Freud said, "Children are completely egoistic; they feel their needs intensely and strive ruthlessly to satisfy them."

The flesh/id wants what it wants now and the spirit/superego is the voice of reason and morality—but how is a decision made on which action to take? According to Freud, that's where the ego comes in and according to Paul, that is the "conflict" he refers to in Galatians 5:17. The ego is the referee between the two. The ego is the mechanism that weighs the costs and benefits of taking a particular course of action or not. In our child example, the ego will decide if the forbidden cookie is eaten or not. The decision may come from the ego to eat half the cookie and put the rest back, or it could decide, "Damn the torpedoes, full speed ahead!" and eat the entire jar of cookies. Whatever the decision, the ego weighs the risks and consequences and makes a decision based upon the risk and reward ratios. According to Galatians 5:17, the reason we have two conflicting natures is so we do not "do whatever we want." When you think about it, it's a fantastic design that God put in place. He created the flesh to desire what keeps us alive and what keeps the species alive, but we have the spirit to guide us and control us to keep us from acting purely on selfish ambition. The net result is a thriving and healthy community. While not perfect, there has been progress as a human race since the beginning of time. If we were purely selfish we would just kill anyone who had what we wanted. However, if we were purely spirit we would never have the desire to do anything because we would not have any desire. Most of that progress is because of this mix of fleshly desires contained and controlled by spirit for the good of the community.

For example, I do not want to work; I do not want to wake up in the morning and crawl out of my bed. I do not want to get ready and be professional at 8:00 AM. However, I do enjoy eating, sleeping in a house, driving a car, and socializing. So while my flesh wants me to enjoy my life in a very leisurely way, my spirit tells me to go to work so I can make money and support the lifestyle to which I have become accustomed and enjoy. How well we do professionally directly benefits our community and directly benefits us as individuals. While a doctor is absolutely essential to the community at large and is essential to keeping people in the community healthy, many doctors are also motivated by the financial rewards of being a doctor. So when a doctor chooses to pursue a degree in medicine, they are benefitting society as well as themselves. The same is true for every profession to varying degrees.

Our spirit, which resides in our brain, is not the same as the Holy Spirit. Our spirit receives the Holy Spirit when we receive Jesus Christ. Let me explain. My television is a receiver of a signal from a television station. The station sends the signal and my television receives the signal and displays it for me on the screen. In a similar manner, God offers us the Holy Spirit, which we choose to receive or not to receive into our minds and hearts. In John 14:16–17, Jesus says,

> *"And I will ask the Father, and he will give you another advocate to help you and be with you forever— the Spirit of truth. The world cannot accept him, because it neither sees him nor knows him. But you know him, for he lives with you and will be in you."*

Everyone has a superego, everyone has a spirit, but not everyone has the Holy Spirit. This is not a value judgment or a criticism; it is simply a statement of fact. Accepting the Holy Spirit is a choice and it is not a choice everyone makes. Everyone on the planet, however, does have a set of values and a set of rules they choose to govern themselves by and Christians are no different. As for me, my spirit is "tuned" to the Holy Spirit and while I fail regularly to live up to His standards, that is what I strive for. Everyone "tunes" their spirit to a channel they choose, and when you know the channel someone has tuned into, you are able to speculate as to what their spirit believes. We refer to these channels as religions. Muslims have a set of values that they see the world through, and their spirit is programmed according to those values. Jews have a set of values they adhere to, and summarily, their spirit is tuned to that set of values; the same is true as with all religions and dogmas. Even people who adhere to no religion have their spirit tuned to something.

Herein lies the problem with many societies. When people tune their spirit into a channel they believe is the correct channel, many believe that channel is correct for everyone. Belief that a channel is correct for everyone is one thing, but unfortunately, throughout the centuries, that belief has led to countless deaths in countless wars. I am a Christian; I believe the God of the Bible created the heavens and the earth and everything and everyone on it. I have many friends who believe differently. This has generated some very heated discussions over the years. Communism is a dogma; so is capitalism. The belief that one is superior to the other is harmless in and of itself; however, the desire to persuade another civilization that one is better than the other has led to wars. The Jews and Muslims have been locked in conflict since Abraham had a child with both Hagar and Sarah in Genesis. Part of my journey to health and happiness was to realize that my spirit is tuned to the Holy Spirit and that He knew what was best for me and that if I concentrated my antenna . . . my prayers, in His direction, He would lead me.

I also realized that my flesh was not evil, my flesh was not "of the devil"; it was just doing what it was designed to do. Our flesh, which is the mammal part of our brain, is designed to keep us alive. It is designed to crave things that keep us alive and keep the species alive. It is designed to crave high-calorie food because we were created in a time when food was hard to come by. It is designed to crave companionship and sex because that is how the species continues. It is designed to crave success and reward successful behavior. Unfortunately, we were designed and built millennia ago, and the rules have changed. We still have a brain that was designed when combat was the way interpersonal disputes were settled. Now we live in a more civilized world where negotiation and compromise rule the day. Subsequently, we cannot, in the modern world, settle who gets the promotion to area manager with swords and shields. We live in a world that was not designed for the people we are. Our society has evolved past the point of what we were designed for. Fortunately, or unfortunately, our flesh is still alive and well within us, and we have to live with it and embrace it, as I did with Slick.

A large part of my healing was to realize that God built me and built me with a flesh and a spirit to serve him by serving others. I had the flesh to motivate me, and I had my spirit to guide me with the guidance of the Holy Spirit. What my struggle taught me was that I had to strengthen my spirit to help me lead my flesh back to a godly and healthy life. My rationale was simple; I believe that the God of the Bible created me. I believe that He sent the Holy Spirit to help me as He promised in John 14:16; therefore, I was created for a reason, and I was not going to end my life before I had served Him. He had promised me in Jeremiah 29:11 that He had plans for me, and if I followed those plans, I would prosper and have hope and a future. I took Him at His word, and it saved my life.

CHAPTER 3

Why Continue?

"He who has a why to live for can bear
almost any how."
—Friedrich Nietzsche

ONE DAY WHILE driving, I was pleading to God for answers. I recalled a verse from Revelations that reads, "During those days' people will seek death but will not find it; they will long to die, but death will elude them" (Revelation 9:6). I was asking myself and God, "Why do I have to keep going?" Ironically, I found the answer to this question in the lyrics of a Motorhead song penned by the great philosopher Lemmy Kilmister. As I was driving, that song came on. It is called "Born to Raise Hell." Within that song there is a line that states, "What are you waiting for? What do you think you were created for?" Knowing full well that God has an awesome sense of humor, I played those words over and over in my mind, "What am I waiting for? What was I created for?" The answer is simple; I have a job to do. The Bible tells us God has a plan for us. In the Old Testament, we read in Jeremiah 29:11, "'For I know the plans I have for you,' declares the Lord, 'plans to prosper you and not to harm you, plans to give you hope and a future.'" This probably sounds incredibly narcissistic, but when I read those words, I felt like Jeremiah wrote them exclusively for me at this time. Of course, I am the guy who gave my subconscious the name Slick, so it shouldn't be

and my life and was actually put there by design. I'm an inquisitive guy by nature; I like things to make sense. What did not make any sense to me is how a relatively good-looking middle-aged guy with a great job and great life can be so miserable that he is contemplating suicide. This made no sense to me at all, so I began to research it and try to find out why. The time had come to get out of the boat and start walking toward Jesus.

CHAPTER 4

We Are Wonderfully Made

"Everything has beauty, but not everyone sees it."
—Confucius

BY NOW YOU have probably realized that I am a Christian, and proud of it. This was not always the case; there were a number of years when God and I were at, shall we say, cross-purposes. We did not always agree on things, mainly because I was having difficulty seeing His handiwork when I was younger. I have come to the realization now that sometimes seeing God's work takes several years and some humble hindsight. I realized that God does not always give us what we need in a chronological order. For example, God equipped me with the make it to midnight experience years before I actually needed it. In John 6:9, God gave the boy the fish hours or even days before he needed it, and when Jesus asked him for it, the boy was prepared to provide it. I think more than anything, seeing repeated examples of how God's work exists outside of the perimeters of time and space convinced me of His existence. Every time I talk with someone about this, they are able to think of an example in which God had prepared them for an event before the event actually happened.

When I was new in the IT industry, I was still navigating the river of life without the faith of a mustard seed. I was making my own way through life, and poorly at that. What I did have was a curiosity that I believe was placed there by God. Everywhere I went, I kept looking around, seeing the complexities of the world around me and could not figure out how this possibly could have just evolved by chance and natural selection. I'm a smart guy; I was a member of Mensa, but I could not reconcile the fact that the world is unimaginably complex, and yet, the greatest scientific minds in the world said it all happened by accident. On one hand, I was taught that everything we see is a product of natural selection and random chance; on the other hand, I was reading that if one component of an ecosystem was removed, the entire system collapsed. How could a complex system evolve if the removal of one piece caused the entire mechanism to collapse?

We were taught in school that matter cannot be created or destroyed, and yet here I am, a giant blob of matter typing on a keyboard made of different matter reading a computer screen made of matter. This quandary led me to start reading books about creation and evolution; after reading several books, I realized that it is impossible for the human race and all the other creatures roaming the planet to not have been created. Some good reads on this are *Darwin's Black Box* by Michael Behe and *The Face That Demonstrates the Farce of Evolution* by Hank Hanegraaff. These and many other books taught me that the human mind is more complex than we are able to imagine; to suggest that it just "evolved" was not only silly, but it was also an enormous insult to whomever created it. I was personally offended, but I got over it. The point is that if you and I are the fantastic works of art that the Bible says we are, then we owe it to ourselves and the artist to honor His creation and to at least give Him one more day. David says in Psalm 139,

> *"For you created my inmost being; you knit me together in my mother's womb. I praise you because I am fearfully and wonderfully made; your works are wonderful; I know that full well. My frame was not hidden from you when I was made in the secret place, when I was woven together in the depths of the earth. Your eyes saw my unformed body; all the*

days ordained for me were written in your book before one of them came to be."

If I was given a new Ferrari, I would not throw it away or run it into a wall because a Ferrari is a valuable car. Recently I watched an episode of *How It's Made: Dream Cars*, which explained what it took to make a Ferrari. It was not the materials that made a Ferrari so valuable; it was the incredible design innovations that went into the car. It was the pride and the craftsmanship that took those raw materials and made an elegant and extremely powerful automobile. After watching that, I wondered what God had to do to make me—what challenges God faced when he designed human beings. I sat on the porch and started a mental exercise to see if I could design life in my own head and the obstacles I would face. Once I started this exercise, I realized exactly what the verse in the Psalm was talking about. After I had just the most basic understanding of the love that it took for God to even consider taking on the task, I no longer felt worthless; I felt like a masterpiece.

The things that we take for granted every day, like hunger and thirst, love and loss, happiness and health, and a thousand others did not "just happen"; God had to create every mechanism for every action and emotion. As humans, we need water, so God created water, and he created thirst to get us to drink. He created hunger to get us to eat. He created love to keep the species alive.

God had to know what we would need *before* we needed it. Not only did He have to know what we needed, but He also had to know when we would need it. He prepared the world for us before He created us. Recently, a renowned physicist, Michio Kaku, concluded that the universe was created by an intelligence rather than random evolution. He said, "I have concluded that we are in a world made by rules created by an intelligence. Believe me, everything that we call chance today won't make sense anymore. To me it is clear that we exist in a plan which is governed by rules that were created, shaped by a universal intelligence, and not by chance."

God created inside of us a very complex system of reward chemicals that keeps us safe, fed, and reproducing. This is called the limbic system. In my journey, the understanding of how the limbic system operated was crucial to my recovery. Realizing that the conflict in my head was not just imaginary or that it was some nebulous "thing," but that there are actual physical components in our brains that work not only independently but in concert with each other was transformational. Unfortunately, mine were working against one another, and it was taking a toll.

God numbered your days and ordained them for you before you were even born. Everything happens for a reason, even you. What I told myself over and over again is that all the things that were happening to me were happening to me for either my benefit or the benefit of someone else. Believe me when I tell you, I have benefitted from my walk through the valley of the shadow of death more than I could have imagined. The bonus is that not only have I benefitted, but others have benefitted from my story . . . hopefully, you are among them. What I know for sure is that if I had pulled the trigger that night and ended my life, I would have assuredly missed the blessings that God had for me. According to Genesis 6:3, God has limited our lifespan to 120 years. Think about that for a moment; God decided thousands of years ago that we would expire after 120 years, that would be our maximum. Despite all the advances in modern medicine and all the wonderful things medical science has given us, our days are numbered to 120 years. If you are going to take this life journey with me, you *have* to resolve to yourself that you are going to persevere to the end. Trust me on this one; the only way you're going to make it to 120 years is if you decide no matter what, that you will always make it to midnight.

I know, in the depths of depression, it's incredibly difficult to see that there is a God and that He cares about you. I know firsthand that when I was at my darkest point, and I stayed there for a long time, I did *not* feel God's presence. What was more impactful was that not only did I not feel God's love, but when people told me that I should feel God's love and I didn't, I felt like a failure. I felt worthless. I remember vividly being really mad at my pastor because he did a series on capturing God's promises for our lives. He told a parable of a widow who was facing starvation, and her creditors were going to take her sons as slaves for payment. She believed in God, but she only had one small jar of oil for payment, and that was not close enough to cover her debts. In the parable, Elisha came and multiplied her oil to such a degree that she was able to never worry about money again. I remember thinking, "Dangit, I believe! Where is my miracle!" God must not love me. I remember seeing all the happy people in church and feeling all the people in the church were getting helped, and here I was, dying inside. Well, I was wrong. God did not give her the oil; God gave her Elisha. I didn't need oil, I needed Elisha, and in that church, I found an army of Elishas. That army of Elishas filled my soul, not my jar. It got me to midnight. One thing that helped me to see I was *not* worthless was to try to see how "wonderfully made" I was. God made you and me. God made us all unique and gave us unique gifts. That army of Elishas filled my soul to such a point that I see those gifts now, and hopefully, I am using them as He intended when He built me.

CHAPTER 5

Slick Gets His Own Room

"Two souls, alas, are housed within my breast, and
each will wrestle for the mastery there."
—Johann Wolfgang von Goethe

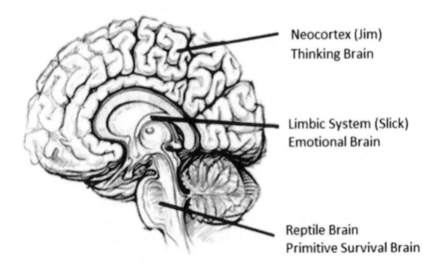

Neocortex (Jim)
Thinking Brain

Limbic System (Slick)
Emotional Brain

Reptile Brain
Primitive Survival Brain

THIS PICTURE ILLUSTRATES the different parts of our brain.
You can see how our brain was developed (or evolved if you prefer).
Reptiles have a survival brain that is primitive; it is designed to sim-
ply keep them alive and reproducing. Mammals are equipped with

the reptile brain as shown above, but they (we) are also equipped with a limbic system, which is the emotional center of the brain. You can see the stark contrast between these brains if you have ever had a reptile as a pet. Reptiles are not affectionate because they do not have a brain built for affection the way mammals do. Finally, in the picture you see the neocortex on top. This is our human brain, our logical brain. I am going to discuss these parts of the brain in greater detail, but hopefully, this picture illustrates that our brain is not just one organ, but a collection of components that make up our entire psyche.

As I learned about Jim, Slick, and the conflict between us, I still did not understand the mechanism behind them because, again, I was under the impression I had one mind, one brain, one organ that was conflicted. This was a contradiction that made very little sense to me. How could one organ, my brain, be in conflict with itself? Our other organs are not in conflict, the heart pumps blood, the digestive organs digest, the spleen does whatever it is a spleen does, but they all do their jobs according to their function, so why would a brain be different? The brain is composed of components that do their jobs to keep the entire organism alive.

As I learned more about neurology, how the brain was constructed, and how all the components of the brain operate, I realized that the "flesh" part of my psyche, which I call Slick, is not just random neurons firing along with other neurons in a unified organ called the brain. Slick is an independent collection of components that work in concert with other components of the brain with the primary purpose of keeping me alive. It is ironic that the emotional center that was designed to keep me alive was telling me to end my life, but that is just part of the complexity of our brain.

One of the unintended benefits of this understanding was that I saw my brain, not as one unit, but as two distinct personalities that resided in the same skull. For those of us that are old enough to remember *The Odd Couple*, you can probably visualize what I am talking about. *The Odd Couple* was a sitcom about two very different men sharing an apartment. Their names were Oscar and Felix. Oscar was a very emotionally-driven sports writer who was very messy and somewhat inconsiderate. Felix, conversely, was a very organized and cerebral news writer who was fairly emotionless and pretty tightly-wound. The comedy of this series was driven by the conflict that was generated by these two men occupying the same apartment. It was humorous because you could see two distinct personalities displayed in two physically separate people. What I discovered and internalized is that the same thing was happening in my brain! After reading several books, attending lectures, auditing college courses online, and doing other research, I found that there are two independent and distinct "brains" contained in my head. There are two distinct thinking mechanisms in our heads and these structures are connected to each other but operate independently. They influence each other but are distinct in their structure.

I will later discuss in greater detail about these components of the organ we collectively call our brain, but for now, just know we have a thinking component of our brain and a feeling component. The thinking component of our brain is the neocortex, which is the essence of who I am as a person, so we will call my neocortex Jim. This is my intellect, my personality; this is the part of my brain that makes me who I am. This part of our brain is responsible for logic and reasoning, it is our "thinking brain." For ease of reading, I am going to refer to this part of my brain as Jim.

The yin to the yang of my thinking brain is the feeling brain, or emotional brain, which I will refer to as Slick. Slick is housed in the structure of our brain called the limbic system. Jim and Slick are completely separate entities that reside in my skull, just like my heart and lungs are separate entities that reside in my chest. My heart has its job of pumping blood and my lungs have their job of oxygenating my blood. Just like my heart depends on my lungs and my lungs depend on my heart to circulate oxygenated blood, Jim and Slick are independent components of a larger system that I call my brain.

There is a third part of our brain that is referred to as the "reptile brain." This is the part of the brain that essentially keeps us alive and functioning. While being alive and functioning is very important to me, the reptile part of my brain is not as integral to my thinking and feeling as Jim and Slick are.

In 1995, a man named Jean-Dominique Bauby had a massive brain stem stroke. This stroke essentially shut off his reptile brain, which left him completely paralyzed and only able to move his left eyelid. In this state, he was unable to speak or move any part of his body or head; his only means of communication was the ability to blink his left eyelid. With that being his only outlet, he dictated a memoir of his experience entitled *The Diving Bell and the Butterfly: A Memoir of Life in Death*. Despite this unfathomable setback, Jean-Dominique Bauby proved through his memoir his determination and ability to live his life as fully in his mind as he did prior to the stroke. He also showed that even when the reptile portion of his brain had been rendered inoperable, his remaining limbic system and neocortex were still able to function unhindered. Bauby died two days after his memoir was published.

While the human mind can continue on if the reptile portion of the brain is eradicated, this is not the case if there is a catastrophic injury to the neocortex or the limbic system. On September 13, 1848, a young man named Phineas Gage was the foreman of a crew cutting railroad bed in Cavendish, Vermont. While he was packing explosive powder into a hole with a metal rod, the powder detonated. The ensuing explosion sent the rod out of the hole with enough velocity to enter Gage's cheek, pass completely through his skull, and land several yards away. According to witnesses, Gage did not appear to have lost consciousness. What is even more incredible is, according to reports, with a 1.25-inch hole in his head, Gage walked to the office of Dr. John Martyn Harlow and said, "Here is business enough for you."

As incredible as it was to believe, Mr. Gage had lost a large chunk of his neocortex. He was still able to speak; however, what Dr. Harlow observed was fascinating. Harlow wrote, "The balance between his intellectual faculties and animal propensities seemed gone." When I read this, my head started spinning, "The *balance* between his intellectual faculties and animal propensities seemed gone." While it is totally unethical to perform an experiment on a human like this, fate had done it for us. His neocortex was all but destroyed and yet he was able to speak and communicate; however, according to people who knew him, he was "no longer Gage." His personality had completely changed. According to his friends, he could not stick to plans, uttered "the grossest profanity," and showed "little deference for his fellows." This is exactly what we would expect if the hypothesis that we have two brains in our head is correct. If our thinking brain is irreparably damaged by an unfortunate accident, then the selfish, emotional side would take over, and that appears to be exactly what happened in the case of Mr. Gage.

Now we have seen the tragic results when there is damage to the spinal cord and the neocortex, but what happens when the limbic system is compromised? Tragically the world got its answer in the form of a young man named Charles Whitman. Charles Whitman was by all appearances the personification of an all-American man. He was tall, blond, former Marine who was studying at the University of Texas to be an architect. Then on July 31, 1966, Charles Whitman went to his mother's apartment and stabbed her and shot her to death. He left a note at the scene, which said that he was "truly sorry that this was the only way I could see to relieve her sufferings but I think it was best." She had left his abusive father years before. He then went home, and after his wife had gone to sleep, he also stabbed her to death leaving a note that read, "I love her dearly . . . I cannot rationally pinpoint any specific reason for doing this."

The following morning, Charles Whitman gathered an assortment of weapons and entered the University of Texas clock tower. After killing the receptionist and two other visitors, Whitman proceeded to the observation deck of the clock tower and began a shooting rampage that lasted just over ninety minutes. The shooting stopped when two police officers fatally shot Whitman. When the smoke cleared, there were fourteen people dead and thirty injured.

While this may sound like nothing more than a deranged man going on a murderous rampage, there is one component that makes this mass shooting different. Every mass murder that I can recall was carried out by a person who had a clear reason for their rage. Some of them were religious, some were frustration, and others, like the Unibomber, were carried out because of frustration with the system. One man recently flew a plane into an IRS building in Austin because he was angry with "Big Government" and the tax system. Charles Whitman was different. Charles Whitman appears to have no idea why he was going to kill all the people he killed. All he knew was that he was compelled by an unrelenting urge to kill.

Prior to the murders, Whitman had visited the university clinic complaining of headaches and telling them, "Recently (I cannot recall when it started) I have been a victim of many unusual and irrational thoughts." Additionally, in his suicide note he wrote, "I do not really understand myself these days. I am supposed to be an average reasonable and intelligent young man. However, lately (I cannot recall when it started) I have been a victim of many unusual and irrational thoughts." Whitman knew something was structurally wrong with his brain, his note continued, "After my death I wish that an autopsy would be performed on me to see if there is any visible physical disorder."

An autopsy was performed on Charles Whitman's brain, and as he had expected, there was a pecan-sized tumor growing in the center of his limbic system. According to Stuart Brown who was an assistant professor of psychology at the Baylor College of Medicine, "The highly malignant brain tumor conceivably could have contributed to his inability to control his emotions and actions."

According to the autopsy, the tumor was growing between the thalamus, hypothalamus, and amygdala. The thalamus is the part of the limbic system that receives sensory input from the various receptors of the body such as the nerves, eyes, or ears. This information is then forwarded to the rest of the brain for processing. The hypothalamus is tasked with taking all the sensory input from the body and maintaining homeostasis. It operates like a thermostat maintaining a constant temperature in a room. The hypothalamus is responsible for the regulation of hunger, thirst, pain, and pleasure levels and appropriate levels of anger and aggression. Finally, the amygdala is the central computer for the fight-or-flight system. When stimulated electrically, the person or animal responds with aggression and rage as if the electrical impulse sends the fight signal. Conversely when the amygdala is removed, the animal will have no emotional response to anything that would normally cause them to express rage or fear.

Experts have debated the role of the tumor in Charles Whitman's brain for over fifty years now. The tumor was pressing on the parts of his brain that regulate and monitor aggression. It is logical to assume that if the tumor was pressing on the part of the hypothalamus that regulated his aggression response as well as pressing on his amygdala, that would be enough to explain his behavior. Having the tumor pressing on the aggression regulation system as well as the system that carries out the aggressive behavior is a deadly combination. Those factors coupled with the fact that Whitman, in his suicide note, admitted that he does not understand his actions, but he has resigned himself to the fact that he is going to carry out those actions. He actually expressed remorse in a note written before he had committed the murders.

In his note, he even goes so far to ask that his life insurance money, if there was any, be donated to a mental health foundation to try and prevent others from doing what he was about to do. That is what strikes me; as he is writing the note, he had committed no crime. He was writing about what he was going to do and he was completely rational. He knew what he was going to do was wrong. He was asking for money to be donated to research his brain to prevent this from happening again, and yet he was unable to stop himself from carrying out the murders. What I believe happened is that the tumor in his limbic system had tipped the scales to the point that he could no longer control his actions. If we read his suicide note through the lens of the two-brain model I propose, we see that while his limbic system and neocortex are in a battle for control, the limbic system has clearly won. A transcript of the suicide note is below.

Sunday
July 31, 1966
6:45 p.m.

I don't quite understand what it is that compels me to type this letter. Perhaps it is to leave some vague reason for the actions I have recently performed. I don't really understand myself these days. I am supposed to be an average reasonable and intelligent young man. However, lately (I can't recall when it started) I have been a victim of many unusual and irrational thoughts. These thoughts constantly recur and it requires a tremendous mental effort to concentrate on useful and progressive tasks. In March when my parents made a physical break I noticed a great deal of stress. I consulted a Dr. Cochrum at the University Health Center and asked him to recommend someone that I could consult with about some psychiatric disorders I felt I had. I talked with a Doctor once for about two hours and tried to convey to him my fears that I felt come overwhelming violent impulses. After one session I never saw the Doctor again, and since then I have been fighting my mental turmoil alone, and seemingly to no avail. After my death I wish that an autopsy would be performed on me to see if there is any visible physical disorder. I have had some tremendous headaches in the past and have consumed two large bottles of Excedrin in the past three months.

It was after much thought that I decided to kill my wife, Kathy, tonight after I pick her up from work at the telephone company. I love her dearly, and she has been as fine a wife to me as any man could ever hope to have. I cannot rationally pinpoint any specific reason for doing this. I don't know whether it is selfishness, or if I don't want her to have to face the embarrassment my actions would surely cause her. At this time, though, the prominent reason in my mind is that I truly do not consider this world worth living in, and am prepared to die, and I do not want to leave her to suffer alone in it. I intend to kill her as painlessly as possible.

Similar reasons provoked me to take my mother's life also. I don't think the poor woman has ever enjoyed life as she is entitled to. She was a simple young woman who married a very possessive and dominating man. All my life as a boy until I ran away from home to join the Marine Corps

[Whitman stopped typing at this point, apparently interrupted by the visit of two friends, who later recalled a "very normal" conversation with Charlie. The note resumes in his handwriting.]

Friends
interrupted
8-1-66

Mon.
3:00 A.M.
Both Dead

I was a witness to her being beaten at least one a month. Then when she took enough my father wanted to fight to keep her below her usual standard of living.

I imagine it appears that I bruttaly [sic] kill [sic] both of my loved ones. I was only trying to do a quick thorough job.

If my life insurance policy is valid, please see that all the worthless checks I wrote this weekend are made good. Please pay off my debts. I am 25 years old and have been financially independent.

Donate the rest anonymously to a mental health foundation. Maybe research can prevent further tragedies of this type.

Charles Whitman
(https://www.popsubculture.com/pop/
bio_project/charles_whitman.html)

What really jumped out to me in Whitman's suicide note was how much I understood how he felt when we wrote, "I don't really understand myself these days. I am supposed to be an average reasonable and intelligent young man. However, lately (I can't recall when it started) I have been a victim of many unusual and irrational thoughts. These thoughts constantly recur and it requires a tremendous mental effort to concentrate on useful and progressive tasks." He knew what he was thinking was wrong, but he was unable to compel himself to stop. He knew that it was completely irrational for him to be having these thoughts as the empirical evidence ("I am supposed to be an average reasonable and intelligent young man") was telling him that he had a fantastic life. If, like the experts tell us, the neocortex is the source of all thoughts, how did a tumor in his limbic system produce "unusual and irrational thoughts?"

His experience and testimony echo what millions of people with suicidal ideation, countless addicts, and what Paul said in Romans 7:15, "I do not understand what I do. For what I want to do I do not do, but what I hate I do." I am by no means painting Charles Whitman as a victim. A group of experts examined Whitman's brain and the tumor and concluded, "The relationship between the brain tumor and Whitman's actions cannot be established with clarity. However, the tumor conceivably could have contributed to his inability to control his emotions and actions." The reason that it cannot be explained with clarity is that scientists did not know as much about the brain as they do now. One thing I have learned in my research is that scientists find very creative ways to say "we don't know." Unfortunately, we never will know. Whitman's brain was disposed of in 2002 along with one hundred other "unusual brains" as the brains had deteriorated to a point that they were no longer usable for research.

CHAPTER 6

Why Do I Feel This Way?

"It's like I have a loaded gun in my mouth
and I like the taste of metal."
—Robert Downey Jr.

WHEN I WAS sixteen, I got my first job in a bar called Studebakers. This bar was amazing and was my first exposure to the bar scene. As the youngest person in the bar, I was immediately everyone's adopted little brother. All the bartenders watched out for me because fights broke out regularly. I was not a large kid; I was a chiseled 125 pounds of rage. The waitresses were amazing as well; they all took an interest in my schoolwork and showered me with dating advice in an effort to make sure I did not turn out like every guy who had done them wrong. While I appreciated their advice, I was working every weekend, so dating was not an issue for me, but their advice did not go unheeded. The patrons were equally wonderful to me; it was like I had an entire team of adults who took a real interest in my well-being.

While I really enjoyed the support and attention of my adopted benefactors, one thing always puzzled me about how so many people could be so smart and so wise, yet keep repeating the same mistakes week after week. These people were not just interested in me because of their good nature; they saw in me a chance to help someone avoid the mistakes they had made in their lives. This is what puzzled me so much; how could these people who had this wonderful advice keep making the same mistakes they warned me not to make? Why did they see me as a chance to correct their mistakes? What was it about my youth that compelled them to see me as *their* second chance to, in some vicarious way, correct the mistakes they had made? These people were no older than forty; they could correct their own mistakes. Why did they feel as if they were doomed to live the rest of their lives that way?

In Greek mythology there is a tale about a man named Sisyphus who was able to outsmart Thanatos—the god of death. According to the story, Sisyphus betrayed Zeus by disclosing the whereabouts of one of Zeus's concubines to her father. When Zeus sent Thanatos (Death) to chain Sisyphus, he outwitted Thanatos and put him in chains instead. As long as Thanatos was in chains, no one on Earth could die. Since no one was able to die, there could be no sacrifice to the gods, which, of course, really upset Zeus. After freeing Thanatos, Zeus felt compelled to not only come up with a suitable punishment for Sisyphus, but he also needed to make the punishment an example to others of what would happen if a mortal disrespected the gods. The punishment that Zeus prescribed to Sisyphus was for him to roll a boulder up a hill every day, just to have it roll to the bottom of the hill again each night. Sisyphus was sentenced to an eternity of hopeless work and toil. Every day he would wake up and push the boulder to the top of the hill with all his energy, just to have it roll to the bottom of the hill every night.

Back at the bar, it was as if all the adults had accepted "Sisyphus's fate" as their own, so they would return to the bar each night and drink themselves to a place where they were numb to their problems. They would then go home, just to wake up and repeat the cycle all over again. I should have trademarked the phrase, "Kid, don't make the mistakes I made." There were many patrons who would come in and say, "Kid, don't ever start drinking." Then they would immediately order another cocktail! Or they would say, "Jim, if I *ever* see you smoking, I'm gonna put that cigarette out on your forehead!" Then they would light another cigarette. This was a night club, so drugs were not hard to come by and the threats against me if I ever tried drugs were much more severe . . . from people who did drugs daily. My young and logical mind was experiencing serious cognitive dissonance. I was hearing people tell me how horrible mind-altering substances are, while, at the same time, watching them partake of those same substances.

I'm a logical guy, and I was young and naïve back then, so I did not understand addictions. I saw the brain like a person driving a car; if I want to go left, I turn left. If I want to go right, then I turn right. Why is this so hard? You have *one* brain, and it is yours; you should be able to make decisions and stick to them . . . or so I thought.

Fortunately, I am not shy, so when I would experience such a dichotomy, I would ask these people, "If you hate smoking so much, why do you still do it?" or "If drinking has cost you your marriage and friends, why do you still drink?" The answer was always the same, "I'd love to quit, but I just can't." My innocent mind constantly questioned, "Why does a person wake up at 8:00 AM with a resolution to never drink or smoke or do drugs and by noon are willing to sell their soul for a fix?" Sisyphus was bound by chains made by gods; his fate was sealed. Yet these people just had to drive home and not come to the bar and stop "pushing their boulder" uphill every night and not have it roll down. They could just walk away from their boulder, be it drugs or alcohol, and leave it behind. At least that's what I thought.

Several years later, I became a bartender at a country bar in Corpus Christi, Texas. On Thursday, Friday, and Saturday nights, I would go to work at 4:00 PM and leave work at 4:00 AM. Like most bartenders, we were not allowed breaks during peak hours because there was always someone at the bar wanting to buy a drink, and there were just enough bartenders to supply the demand. In the bar I worked in, like most bars, smoke breaks were allowed, and since the managers were smokers, they knew what the business end of a nicotine fit was like, so they allowed smoke breaks as an exception. In my mind, I was still hearing my old friends from Studebakers chastising me every time I thought about taking up the habit, but sadly, one night I jumped on the bandwagon and began smoking. It was a perfect-storm scenario; it was a very busy night with several fights to break up, and I was not in a good mood. It was then that an angelic figure appeared at my bar through the smoky haze with a tray filled with free sample packs of cigarettes. This was the nineties, so smoking was still not much of a taboo. Anyway, I looked at the angel (of death!) and said, "Yes, ma'am, I am a smoker, thank you." She then handed me a pack of cigarettes, and I took my first of what would be thousands of smoke breaks. At first, as you can imagine, I was not graceful in my smoking; I was coughing and wheezing as if my body had been poisoned, using every muscle at its disposal to rid my lungs of this foreign toxin . . . probably because that's exactly what was going on. However, with dogged perseverance, I became a smoker and really liked it. I had unwittingly fastened my own chains and had begun my journey in the footsteps of Sisyphus.

It was not until several months later that I realized I had become addicted to cigarettes. Upon realizing that I was now hooked, that nagging question came to me again, "How can I want to not smoke, but at the same time have a truly overwhelming desire to smoke?" The desire was so strong I was unable to think of anything else. It was about this time that I learned about an experiment that scientists had done with monkeys that had become addicted to nicotine. The addicted monkeys turned down food and sex for nicotine. I saw myself in those monkeys. The monkeys were living what I was feeling; the monkeys had no concept of addiction. All they knew is that they wanted nicotine! Again, I came back to the same question, "Why, when I decided to quit at eight o'clock in the morning, am I climbing the walls for a cigarette by noon?" I had become addicted to cigarettes, and this was causing a daily conflict within me—whether to continue smoking or not. I knew the health risks of smoking, but there was a prominent part of me that didn't care. It was as if I had one part of my brain that wanted to quit and another part that said, "Shut up and give me a damn cigarette!" It was as if I, Jim, was not a smoker, but Slick really liked cigarettes. Because we were not in agreement on smoking, we had a conflict. At this point in my life, I did not have a good understanding of the brain, so I could not see what is now so obvious. We do not just have one brain.

Let's go back to Studebakers. There were people there who were addicted to alcohol. Like Sisyphus, they were pushing that boulder of the hill of alcoholism every day, just to start the process over each morning. Those people would come in every day after work and sit at the bar and drink until they were tired, then they would go home. They did not particularly enjoy the club or the alcohol, but they were compelled to come there every day. Without exception, as the night went on, they would tell me about the horrors of alcohol and how I should never start drinking. Every one of them would tell me not to start drinking because they were addicted and were unable to stop, and they did not want the same fate for me.

In Luke 16:19–31, Jesus tells the story of a rich man and a poor man who both died. In the parable, the rich man went to Hades where he was to be tormented with fire for eternity. The rich man begged from the torment of Hades that someone would go tell his relatives of his agony so they would repent and turn from their sins. He was told that if they had not listened to Moses and the prophets, they would not be convinced by someone returning from the dead either. The point of the parable, in this context, is that even though we see the damage that is done by alcohol and drugs, we do not take it to heart until we experience it, and then it is too late. Our neocortex knows that alcohol can lead to addiction, but until our limbic system becomes addicted, we do not realize what it means. I use this parable to further illustrate the point that we have two distinct components in our psyche, an emotional component and a logical component.

Today, we see the pictures of what an addict looks like after years of hard drug use; they look terrible, yet these pictures do not dissuade younger people from using drugs. Something about our thinking brain tells us that we are immune to the effects of whatever drug or substance is being abused. It is not until they experience the effects of drugs that they realize the trap they are in. I felt as if this was almost the same thing that was happening in the bar every night. These people who were at the bar felt there was no hope for them, that they had been relegated to a life of alcoholism. They would joke, "What's the difference between an alcoholic and a drunk? Drunks don't go to meetings!" Yet while they had accepted their position at the bar, they were desperately trying to warn me not to follow in their footsteps before it was too late. Again, if they did not have two personalities, they would stop coming to the bar.

What they were really saying was, "When I was your age, I did not drink, and after I started drinking, I was unable to stop." They knew alcohol was potentially bad for them, but it was not until they *experienced* it that they could not stop. In my case, my thinking brain knew what alcohol was, but my limbic system did not; once my feeling brain experienced the effects of alcohol, *it* would not let me stop. Their limbic system liked the feeling alcohol provided and it became the crying baby in their head that would not be silenced until it had a drink. So in essence, they were telling me not to introduce Slick to alcohol. I obviously knew what alcohol was, but Slick did not, and *that* was why they were trying to save me from their fate. They saw in me a second chance because once their "Slick" had tasted and experienced alcohol, their fate was sealed. Their neocortex was warning my neocortex not to pick up a drink, and fortunately, I listened long enough to understand the effects of alcohol, and we (Slick and I) were prepared. *This*, ladies and gentlemen, is why we have a minimum drinking age. Our neocortex is not fully developed until our early twenties; the decision to partake in mind-altering substances should be postponed until then.

To recap, we are born with an almost exclusive limbic brain. Our brain, for the first few years of life, is strictly emotional; there is very little logic. As we age and become adolescents, we start to develop our neocortex. This is the brain that learns the rules and understands that actions have consequences. As we hit our early twenties, these two brains become equal partners in our head.

Imagine, if you will, you have three people in a car. The driver represents our reptile brain. The driver is responsible for driving the car, maintaining and monitoring the car, and getting the passengers to their destination. In the back seat of the car, you have a father and a son. The father, who is our neocortex, has hired the driver to drive the two of them across the country to a meeting. The father knows two things: he knows that his meeting is in two days and they have sixteen-hour drive to get there. The father has planned out that they will drive eight hours per day to reach their destination. They have just left on the first day. The son, however, is a typical six-year-old boy, and he represents our limbic system. He knows he's going on a trip and he is glued to the window of the car looking at the landscape pass by. He is living in the moment, unconcerned about his father's meeting or the destination; all he knows is that he is on a trip with his dad, so he is safe and happy.

The example above is how the brain should work. We have the three parts of our brain: the father is the thinking brain, the son is the feeling brain, and the driver is the reptile brain. At the most basic level, the goal of all three parts of the brain is simple; stay alive. The most basic job of the driver is to keep the car (the body) functioning and keep the occupants inside the car safe. The driver carefully watches the gauges to make sure that everything is operating properly in the vehicle. He regulates the heat and air-conditioning to keep the occupants comfortable and he navigates the course set by the father to get to the destination on time. He follows the father's directions as far as time and speed for arrival.

The other job of the driver is to avoid danger and keep the passengers safe from harm. If there is an obstruction on the road, the driver will avoid it. Similarly, if there is danger to our survival, the survival brain is equipped with the "fight, flight, or freeze" mechanism. This mechanism is stored in the survival brain for the simple reason that the decision on what to do needs to happen without debate; it needs to be instinctive. If you have ever seen a sea turtle just minutes after it hatches, it immediately moves as quickly as it can toward the water. The turtle has no idea why it is doing this because sea turtles don't have ideas; they just live on the instinct to survive. However, when God created sea turtles, He knew that He also created birds who like to eat sea turtles as well as other predators. Because these predators would see a newborn sea turtle as an easy meal, God programmed the DNA for turtles to compel them to get to the water immediately after birth where it has a better chance of survival. Our survival brain operates the same way, it just does what it does to survive, and we hope the decision is the correct one.

The father in this scenario is the neocortex or thinking brain, and we will call him Neil. His job is to tell the driver where to go to reach his meeting on time. This is the brain that understands concepts like past, present, and future and he uses words like "should" to determine its course of action. Neil knows all the rules and determines how to follow the rules and accomplish the task he has at hand. He is unconcerned with the landscape or where the world's largest ball of yarn is on the journey; he has a task to perform—getting to the meeting. Neil is logical, electrical, and unemotional. He has a good job and knows that if he does not show up for this meeting, his job will be in jeopardy, so he will do whatever is necessary to get to the meeting on time. He knows that his job is contingent upon his performance, so showing up to the meeting late or not at all is not an option for him. He is the executive of the brain.

Prior to my understanding of the brain, I thought that the interactions between the mind and body were simple; the brain tells the body what to do, and the body obeys. To continue the metaphor, I assumed the driver worked for Neil, so in order to arrive at his meeting on time, the father tells the driver how fast to drive, which route to take, and what the destination is for that day. The decision was made and the orders were carried out. The system is symbiotic and elegant, and for many people, this is how they assume our brains work. I know I did. I thought that once a decision was made, the body and mind carried out that decision. I think that is the assumption that most people have about the brain.

This assumption leads to an unavoidable conclusion that when a person makes a decision to do something, such as to stop an addictive behavior, and they fail, it is because of weakness. In my mind, addicts were weak; people who stayed in abusive relationships were weak, people who didn't work were weak, everyone who did not handle a situation the way I would was weak. I was wrong. Addicts are not weak; it is their limbic system conflicting with their neocortex on whether to carry out the addictive behavior or not. Most of the time the spirit wins, but sometimes the flesh will win, and that's when you have a relapse.

We have not addressed the child in the car, but we will metaphorically put him in the back seat for a moment. Let's just look at what we have so far. We have a man, Neil, who is attending a meeting in two days and we have a driver who has been hired to get him there. Seems simple and complete. The man logically decides the route, the driver carries out the task, and at the end of the second day, they arrive on time, barring an accident or a malfunction in the car. In this case, we have a logical center of the brain and we have the body that carries out these tasks; sounds about right—but it is not. If this were all there were to our brains, then when we decided to do something, we would do it. Paul illustrates this point beautifully in Romans 7:15 when he says,

> *"I don't really understand myself, for I want to do what is right, but I don't do it. Instead, I do what I hate."*

Does this passage sound familiar to anyone? How about everyone. We are taught we have a brain and the brain makes decisions, and our bodies follow those decisions, or should follow them, but they do not. This is the source of Paul's confusion, and the confusion of every human being before and since. At its essence, what is sin? When Paul says in Romans 7:15 he wants to do what is right, the fact that he does not have to expound on "what is right" presupposes that everyone is in agreement to what is "right." Also in Galatians 5:17, Paul says the spirit and the flesh are in conflict with each other so you cannot do "whatever you want." This statement assumes that what we want to do is contrary to what is right, and it further presupposes that we all agree upon what is right, which, for the most part, is correct. Obviously, there are outliers in this presupposition, but society, as a whole, falls in line with what God outlined in the Ten Commandments. Even the most basic society has to establish rules that become in that society the definition of what is right. Whether you agree with the Ten Commandments or not, even societies that were completely ignorant of them established rules that were similar; if they had not, those societies would no longer exist.

So why is it that we want to do what is right but we seem to be unable to? The simple answer is that there is a little kid riding along with us and that little kid who represents our limbic system is the reason we stray from the right path. Continuing with the car ride analogy, we see that Neil the Neocortex has set forth a path to his meeting; he instructs the driver to follow the course laid out in the time allotted, and by doing so, they will arrive to the meeting on time. What if on this journey, the child sitting next to the father sees a sign that says "Wildlife Park 10 miles ahead"? At this point, the child who represents the limbic system, who we will call Lucas, tells his father that he wants to stop and see the animals. Predictably, Neil tells Lucas, "No." Neil reasons that if he stops at the wildlife park, it will throw off their schedule, and he will be late for his meeting. Herein lies the impasse. Lucas wants to stop and see the animals, and Neil knows that he has responsibilities that require him to keep driving. The negotiation between the two is what we deal with every day of our lives.

As you can imagine, the news of Neil not allowing Lucas to go to the wildlife park is met with strong resistance. Now Lucas has a dilemma, as his father does have veto power, and he does tell the driver where to go. Lucas wants to see the animals, so he must find a way to get his father to change his mind and allow him to go to the wildlife park. From a purely emotional point of view, what are Lucas's options? Knowing full well he cannot reason with his father, Lucas now decides to throw a tantrum in the back seat. He decides he is going to make his father increasingly uncomfortable until his father relents and allows him to see the wildlife park. He has seen animals in the zoo before, and he likes animals. Here is what he perceives as a once-in-a-lifetime opportunity to see his favorite animals up close and so to him, the "no" is not an option. In the midst of the tantrum, Lucas has now made Neil and the driver absolutely miserable. He is now kicking and screaming; he is causing the driver (the brain stem) to become agitated, and he is damaging the car (the body).

Lucas's continued screams and thrashing about have led to a very uncomfortable ride for everyone. After a couple of miles, his father has come to a very discouraging realization; he is in a no-win situation. If he says yes to his Lucas, he will have reinforced in the son that throwing a tantrum is the way to get what he wants, and he will be late for his meeting. Neil feels he needs to maintain his authority in the relationship. He also realizes that if he does not stop at the wildlife park, not only will the next five miles be miserable, but the entirety of the trip will be miserable because the tantrum will continue well past the exit for the wildlife park. The father has now come to grips with the fact that no matter what he chooses, it is not the right choice, as the right choice is to drive on and get to the meeting on time.

Finally, after spending another few miles at the business end of his son's hissy fit, Neil relents and instructs the driver to go to the wildlife park. He rationalizes that he can make up the time later. He realizes that the driver will be fatigued, and he will have to pay the driver extra for the stop and the extended time behind the wheel. He logically weighs the costs and benefits of the decision and allows his son to see the animals. The son is temporarily satisfied . . . until the next roadside attraction catches his eye.

This little scenario is what takes place in our brains every day. Our logical brain knows what it "should" do. However, our emotional brain (Lucas) has an idea of what he wants to do and, in this scenario, is not what Neil wants to do and honestly believes he needs to do. This simple illustration shows the conflict that Paul was talking about in Galatians and that Freud talked about with the id (Lucas) and the superego (Neil). *This* is the root of most of the problems I experienced and the root of a myriad of other problems other people face. This is the root of addiction and all undesired behaviors. Our limbic system was designed to avoid pain and seek pleasure. If it finds a way to find pleasure, be it a substance or an activity, that is exactly what it will do. That is what cravings are; they are our limbic system's way of trying to seek pleasure. If the desire is strong enough, it becomes an addiction. Just like the kid throwing a tantrum and damaging the car in the scenario, our limbic system will wreak havoc on our bodies in order to get what it wants. When it craves something, it will make the neocortex, and the body as miserable as possible in order to meet its needs.

We are told that as we mature we become adults. The prevailing wisdom is that our child brain is replaced with an adult brain. The Bible says, "When I was a child, I talked like a child, I thought like a child, I reasoned like a child. When I became a man, I put the ways of childhood behind me" (1 Corinthians 13:11). What I am proposing is that the child brain remains and the adult brain grows on top of it. These two brains exist in parallel and compete for control. We never really "become adults"; we just acquire a logical brain that is cognizant of right and wrong. One day, we wake up and start using the word "should." People who suffer with anxiety and depression tend to worry more about how their actions or inactions will affect others, or what others will think about them. "I should be further in my career", "I should volunteer even though I am tired," "I should not tell people how I am really feeling." In an attempt to mitigate this, I try to worry less about what other people will think and concentrate more on what Slick will feel.

CHAPTER 7

Not Built for This World

"Everyone is a genius. But if you judge a fish by
its ability to climb a tree, it will live its whole
life believing that it is stupid."
—Albert Einstein

WE WERE CREATED millennia ago. We were created to hunt, eat, reproduce, and survive. Our primary function was day-to-day survival. Dangers faced at that time included disease, injury, tribal warfare, and lack of food. Our dangers were immediate and real threats to our existence, both individually and collectively. The dangers we faced were generally short in duration, and there was a good chance we would not survive those challenges in many cases. God built in us mechanisms that protect us from these dangers. The limbic system is that mechanism. The limbic system is comprised of components and chemicals to help us fight or flee dangerous situations. It helps us to identify and categorize which situations are legitimate threats and which are not. It is equipped with mechanisms to allow us to not only learn from our experiences but the experiences of others.

What our limbic system is *not* equipped for are the challenges we face in the twenty-first century. We are not built to live in the world we live in currently. We are not built to have mortgages and car payments, yet we have them. We are not built to deal with revolving credit card debt or insurance payments, medical bills, electric bills, property taxes, daycare expenses, and all the other things that we find in our mailboxes each month. We were built to survive each day. The Lord's Prayer says clearly, "Give us this day our daily bread." In Exodus chapter 16, God sends manna from heaven. He commands the Israelites to only collect enough manna for each day. Then the Lord said to Moses, "Look, I'm going to rain down food from heaven for you. Each day the people can go out and pick up as much food as they need for that day. I will test them in this to see whether or not they will follow my instructions. On the sixth day they will gather food, and when they prepare it, there will be twice as much as usual." (Exodus 16:4-5). When some of the Israelites disobeyed, they found the food to be rotten: "But some of them didn't listen and kept some of it until morning. But by then it was full of maggots and had a terrible smell. Moses was very angry with them" (Exodus 16:20).

Many people, myself included, sign thirty-year mortgages on our homes. We sign a piece of paper that obligates us to pay someone a set amount each month or we will lose our home. The mortgage does not state, "As long as you have a job and have no illnesses you must pay this mortgage." Each month, I get an envelope in the mail that has a fairly large number in the blank that says "Payment Amount." This prolonged Chinese water-torture type of stress takes a toll on people. Like the old joke says, "I owe, I owe so it's off to work I go." We were not built for this kind of stress.

Another kind of stress that we face today that we are not built for is the 24-7 nature of our world. God designed us with a specific rhythm that is synchronized with the cycle of the twenty-four-hour day. We were built to wake when the sun comes up and rest when the sun goes down. Now, with the internet, there are no time zones. With the advent of modern communication technology, there is no longer a day or night. We can be contacted at any time.

Another example of how our brains were not built for the world we live in that hits close to home is dieting. I recently went on a whole food diet; essentially, I could eat or drink nothing processed. Have you ever wondered why foods taste the way they do? I have. What is important to realize is that we were built in a time when survival was not easy. There were no grocery stores thousands of years ago and finding food was a different level of commitment. Today, we count calories because we have too many available. Thousands of years ago, even hundreds of years ago, survival was difficult. The formula was simple; the more calories you ate, the more likely you were to survive. God designed our limbic system so God had to motivate us to eat higher-calorie foods to have a better chance of survival . . . so he made them taste good. In our modern world we drive by grocery stores and restaurants every day. For us, we no longer need to fight for calories; we find that we need to reduce our calorie intake to maintain our health because calories are too easy to come by.

Having visited grocery stores countless times in my life, I knew all the foods I could eat on my whole food diet would be on the perimeter of the store. The meat section is in the back, the eggs are on the west wall, and the vegetables and fruits are on the east wall. Simple enough to remember, but out of habit, my brain stem walked toward the cereal aisle. While your neocortex and limbic system are fighting it out over what to do, your brain stem is driving the bus. That is why you can drive to and from work and not remember the trip, because, while your higher functioning brain is pondering life's choices, your brain stem is keeping all your parts working and moving in the right direction.

I currently have no noteworthy addictions, but I do love me some Cinnamon Toast Crunch. So as I am walking leisurely down the cereal aisle, I snap back to reality and realize where I am. I am six days into a healthy food diet and I am staring at a huge box of Cinnamon Toast Crunch! And yes, God did make Cinnamon Toast Crunch. Again, we flash back to the highway and the father and son. My primitive emotional brain begins throwing the mother of all tantrums because we are still operating in bodies that were designed when food ran away from us. A stationary high-calorie treat like Cinnamon Toast Crunch was too good to pass up, but I was prepared, and I walked away. Fortunately, my thinking brain won this battle. This again illustrates the point that we were not built to live in the world we live in. We were built in a time when obesity was nonexistent and calories were very difficult to come by.

It is hard for us today to comprehend the world that our ancestors lived in. Every day they had to go find food, and when I say find food, I do not mean at the store; they actually had to either pick, cut, or kill what they ate. There was no refrigeration and there was no sanitation, so the option of stocking food in the freezer was not an option available to them. People also lived in communities of varying sizes for protection. Our ancestors lived in less-than-hospitable circumstances. Not only did they have to get along with the members of their community to produce positive outcomes for the community; they also had to protect themselves from members of other communities who sought to do them harm. The best example of this is the TV series *The Walking Dead*. That show illustrates perfectly what is it is like to live with a group and the consequences of being alone. We see in Genesis 21 where Hagar and Ishmael were sent away from Abraham's camp and that exile was essentially a death sentence. For our ancestors, life was decidedly more difficult, and our bodies and minds were designed to keep us alive in a harsh environment. Now that we live in a world that is almost devoid of life and death struggles, our brains have not quite adjusted.

First and foremost, we were created by God for the primary purpose of survival. We were not built to be happy or content; we were built to survive. If you think of the Lord's Prayer, "Give us this day our *daily* bread," not give us all the bread we need for a month, then we can chill and watch TV. We were built to work and achieve. We were built with a reward system in our brains, a system that rewards success . . . success that, by its very definition, requires action. If you do nothing then success is not possible, you have to do *something* to be rewarded. The reward that God built into us was the chemicals in our limbic system. If you find food, you are rewarded, if you find a mate you are rewarded, if you accomplish something positive for the group or yourself, you are rewarded.

When we were created, everything was a struggle. Finding food was a struggle; now we have fast food. Throughout human history finding a mate was a struggle; now we have dating websites. For our ancestors, evading predators, either animal or human, was a struggle; and now we hunt for sport. From the beginning of time survival was a struggle. Electricity was not placed in homes until the early 1920s, which is less than a hundred years ago. Our ancestors fought to survive every day, and those who survived were rewarded for their efforts. These rewards are taken for granted by most of us because we never really think about them. For example, I love doughnuts . . . *love* doughnuts. I was on a trip to Japan recently and a man was wearing a jacket that had "Donuts" written on the back of it. I have no idea why, but it was awesome. I wanted that jacket but never found another one . . . but I digress. Doughnuts are delicious, but high in calories. Candy is delicious and high in calories; broccoli is not delicious and not high in calories. Ever notice that things that are high in calories are generally delicious? Why is that? Because thousands of years ago when calories were very hard to come by, we were built to crave foods with high calories. More calories meant a better chance of survival. So God, being smart, made things with high calories taste good. Think about that, God wanted us to survive; calories equal survival, so he created an ingenious way to get us to eat high-calorie foods. He made them delicious.

In economics, there is a concept called the law of diminishing marginal utility. It states that as a person increases consumption of a product while keeping consumption of other products constant, there is a decline in the benefit that person derives from consuming each additional unit of that product. Calories are an excellent example of how our species has "evolved" past the point and is proving the law of diminishing marginal utility. The average human needs to consume two thousand calories a day just to maintain their weight and health. This assumes their daily activity burns two thousand calories per day. Assuming their calories consumed and calories burned equal each other, in this case two thousand per day, then they will maintain homeostasis. In this scenario, we have two variables, calories consumed and calories burned. Thousands or millions of years ago, when human beings were first created, we had to work very hard to find two thousand calories in a day. This search for calories involved hunting, fishing, gathering, scavenging, and whatever means we have at our disposal to find food. To make matters worse, the quest for food actually caused us to burn more calories, which further exacerbated our extant problem of not having enough calories. The point is, for all of human history up to the last hundred years or so, calories were not in surplus.

Fast forward to the present day, and we have the opposite problem. We have access to too many calories. If I want to eat ten thousand calories, I only need to go to the store on the corner and raid the candy aisle. This is diminishing marginal utility in action. Every calorie that exceeds two thousand for me is a calorie that will reduce the benefit of the food I eat. My point is that humans were not built to live in the world we live in now, and we must acknowledge that fact so we can set appropriate expectations for ourselves and others. Humans were designed to spend their day searching for their "daily bread." However, today the hunt for food will consume none of my time as I will just go to whatever store or restaurant I choose and get the food I want.

You may be asking yourself, "Why are you talking about dieting in a book about mental illness?" The simple answer is, cravings are cravings, and they all spring from the same place—our limbic system. Some cravings, like food, are relatively harmless; but others, when satisfied, can have effects that last a lifetime. My years spent bartending were some of the best of my life. The conversations that float across a bar are extremely entertaining, especially as the night wears on. Without question, weeknights are when the best conversations happen because the music is not very loud, and the people who are there on a Tuesday or Wednesday are usually regulars. One night, one of my regulars came in, sat at the bar, and said, "Jim, sex is like a bank account . . . as soon as I withdraw, I lose interest." The first round that night was on me. While that is a pretty horrible joke, what he said makes a lot of sense through the two brain lens. His limbic system wanted sex. It did not really care from whom; it just wanted to be satisfied. Once it was satisfied and the tantrum was over, so was the craving, and his interest in the person with whom he had just had sex.

The joy of sex was designed as a reward for reproducing. However, in our modern world, with the advent of birth control, now we can have sex just for the reward of the good feelings it produces. This is again an example of how we still have a limbic system that was designed millennia before the technology of our current culture evolved. I have seen it countless times; people who knew they were no good for each other would go home together after a night of drinking, and sometimes before the drinking. They would go home together because they both craved sex. They both had a limbic system that was craving the reward chemicals that sexual contact releases. This seemingly irrational behavior is not restricted to bars either. This behavior happens every day in offices where a man and woman have a clandestine meeting and then afterward immediately regret it. There are countless examples, but why does this happen? Let's take my friend at the bar for example. We'll call him Jeff. Jeff had a penchant for meeting women and talking them into going home with him; he was a good-looking, charismatic guy who had the gift of gab and women were very attracted to that. What confused me about Jeff is that he was frustrated that he could not find a girlfriend, which is what he really wanted. He would meet a woman, take her home with him or maybe go on a date or two, and then completely lose interest after they slept together.

It is my hypothesis that Jeff's limbic system was steering him toward women it was attracted to physically. So if his limbic brain is very attracted to a woman (and remember, the limbic brain only wants what it wants now), it will scream and yell until it has its craving satisfied. However, once it is satisfied, the limbic brain shuts off and will go quiet, and the thinking brain is left to deal with the consequences. Every time I talked to him, it was the same story. He'd meet a lady, and usually after a few drinks, they would talk and dance, and then more often than not, they would leave the bar together. He would tell me that he was genuinely interested in the woman he was talking to and was not a "player." He said he would really like a relationship, but as soon as they slept together, his interest would disappear and all he wanted was for them to leave. So why is this? The simple answer is that his limbic brain wanted sex. His neocortex wanted a relationship, and his way of reconciling this was to meet women at the bar. The problem for him is that he would approach, meet, and spend the evening with women that his limbic brain was attracted to. His neocortex was not involved in the process; as soon as he slept with these women, his limbic system had the chemicals it craved. It would go silent, leaving his thinking brain lying there with a complete stranger. This would then be an awkward situation and explains why he wanted them to leave.

What essentially was happening was that his limbic system was craving the neurochemicals that are released when he had sex. Sex doesn't feel good for its own sake; God made sex feel good as a reward for doing a desired behavior, which is reproducing. Jeff's limbic system had found that he could get the reward of the chemicals his brain produced by meeting women at the bar who were willing to sleep with him. Unfortunately for Jeff, his thinking brain was looking for a woman who it connected with on an intellectual level. This makes total sense if you think about it; if his limbic brain and her limbic brain were attracted to one another, they didn't need to consult their thinking brains because they were attracted on an "animalistic" level. They both wanted the reward chemicals sex produced, and the decision was made. After years of playing this game, Jeff was able to identify women who would most likely sleep with him the night they met. After watching Jeff for a while, I suggested that he not sleep with a woman for the first month they knew each other. That would give his thinking brain time to get to know her thinking brain and see if they were compatible. That lasted about a week.

Now let's discuss the flip side of this scenario. What about the women who ended up with Jeff, why did they end up with him? For every Jeff, there is a corresponding Jennifer. I have seen this scenario play out my entire life; women will tell me, or say it on social media, or I will overhear it, "Why can't I meet a nice guy? I keep ending up with jerks!" Then you see them a few weeks later, and guess what? They have found yet another jerk. Again, the answer is simple; their limbic brain is attracted to the "bad boy" and the reasons for that are debated wildly, but the prevailing theory is that women want the alpha male in the tribe because he is generally the most confident. That, coupled with the fact that she knows Jeff is desired by other women, makes him, by definition, the most desirable male. While her neocortex knows that this is a bad way to judge men, her limbic system sees it as completely rational because it was designed during a time when having the strongest male meant she had a much better chance for survival for her and her children.

The scenario plays out like this; Jennifer knows that Jeff has cycled through women like a subway turnstile. Her thinking brain knows that she will more than likely be just another one of those, but one fateful night, she and Jeff cross paths and the inevitable happens. His limbic brain takes control; he is charming and attractive, and because of years of experience, he knows exactly what to say to her limbic brain. A few drinks and a few hours later, they are lying in bed after having sex as virtual strangers. When both of their brains have the chemicals they craved, they lay there in awkward silence until one of them decides it's time to go home.

Why does this normally happen in bars? Is it the social aspect or is it the alcohol? The simple answer is both. If my hypothesis is correct and the thinking brain lives in the neocortex and the emotional brain lives in the limbic system, then alcohol is the primary reason this occurs. Social situations happen all the time, but one-night stands are generally relegated to a night at the bar. Alcohol is a unique drug in that it causes the body to shut down systems to protect itself. The systems in the body are prioritized in order of necessity. So if we look at the brain from the base of the brain stem outward, we see the order that alcohol shuts down these systems in order to protect the body and brain:

Intellect (Jim)
(The Neocortex)

Emotion (Slick)
(The Limbic System)

Motor Functions (Reptile Brain)
(Walking, Talking, Driving, The Brain Stem)

Semi-voluntary (Reptile Brain)
(Blinking, Swallowing, The Brain Stem)

Involuntary (Reptile Brain)
(Gastrointestinal System, Reproductive System, The Brain Stem)

Vital (Reptile Brain)
(Heart, Respiration, The Brain Stem)
Source: Texas LCDC Study Guide

From the list above, we see that in order to protect the body and brain from the effects of alcohol, the first system to shut down is the intellect, i.e., the neocortex. So when the intellect shuts down, guess what takes over? The emotional brain. The emotional brain has poor judgment in that it has no concept of the consequences of its actions, nor does it care. After a couple of drinks, intellect has been shut down, the emotions take over. If you have ever been around drunk people, or if you have been drunk, you have seen this firsthand. Obviously, poor decision making and allowing the limbic system to make decisions that are not in the best interest of the person, as a whole, is not something that happens exclusively with the consumption of alcohol. Alcohol does allow us to see what happens when the thinking brain is rendered inert. The downside is that alcohol intoxication wears off, and on the following morning, when the neocortex is brought back, the consequences of the previous night remain. This can be seen most clearly when someone believes that after a few drinks they are still able to drive, but they are tragically proven wrong.

This simple diagram helps to explain alcoholism. Adhering to the two-brain model, we can see how a limbic system that craves alcohol can overpower a neocortex that knows drinking in not in the best interest of the person who struggles with alcohol. My favorite definition of an alcoholic is "Someone who cannot accurately predict what will happen after they take their first drink." The reason I like this definition is that it explains the process of how the limbic system can make a person uncomfortable through withdrawals or constant craving to the point that their resolve weakens and they take their first drink. Referring to the table above, we see that the first thing to be disabled upon the consumption of alcohol is the neocortex.

If I were someone who struggled with alcoholism, the scenario would play out like this: Let's assume that I had a bad day at work and came home and sat on the couch. Slick would then start putting the thought in my head to go to the kitchen and get a drink. Jim (my neocortex) would say, "I better not, bad things happen when I drink." As the minutes ticked by, Slick would become increasingly agitated and begin to start to remind me how good a beer would taste. He might even start making me crave foods that go well with beer, like pizza or hamburgers. Slick would start painting scenarios of me relaxing with a beer. What he would be doing is inflicting discomfort. This discomfort will lead to mild anxiety . . . or if I were a heavy drinker, it could lead to major anxiety.

Every problem consists of two parts: the activating event and whether you care about it or not. If one of these parts is missing, then the problem doesn't exist. If I do not have money for rent, that is a problem . . . but it is a problem only if I care. If I do not care whether I live in a house or not, then it is not a problem. If I am confronted with the inability to pay rent, then my neocortex, being logical, will work day and night to formulate a solution to this dilemma. At some point, Slick will become exhausted from the stress that comes with trying to find rent money. What he will do is look for ways to silence my neocortex. Alcohol does exactly that; it disables the thinking part of the brain. Knowing this, Slick will then start the process of having me crave alcohol, thereby making my neocortex stop thinking about rent. The activating event, lack of money for rent, is still there, but since I no longer care, it is no longer a problem. The logical neocortex wants to solve the problem by making the activating event go away. Slick wants to solve the problem by making the feelings of anxiety go away.

When some of my clients have a problem they want to address, I ask them the question, "Do you want me to fix it or do you want me to listen?" By asking this question, I am essentially saying, "Do you want me to talk to your neocortex or your limbic system?" In doing this, I am asking them if they want me to fix their problem or validate their feelings. The answer to that question directs our conversation so that I can provide them the maximum benefit. Let's say a client comes into my office and says, "I'm having trouble coping with my job search." My response would be, "Would you like me to help you with that problem, or would you like me to listen." By asking this question, I am, in essence, asking her, "Would you like me to talk to your thinking brain or your emotional brain? If she says I would like you to help me fix it, I would talk to her thinking brain and suggest various job websites and recruiters.

One night in Phoenix, Arizona, dozens of school bus windshields had been smashed. From all appearances, this was the work of vandals. The police wrote the incident off as "kids just being kids." A few months later, the incident was repeated, and on that night, seventy-nine school bus windshields were broken. A police investigation uncovered that a man who owned a windshield repair business had hired people to smash the bus windshields. The business owner created a problem (the broken windshields), then *he* provided a solution. This is not unlike what happens in the limbic system of an addict. The limbic system will cause withdrawal symptoms such as shakes, headaches, sweats, and anxiety to create a problem, then it will generate cravings as a proposed solution. Their "Slick" will make them increasingly uncomfortable until they relent and take a drink, thereby attaining what he wants—alcohol. In the addict, as well as someone like me, who struggled with suicidal ideation, that voice in our heads can be a very powerful and persuasive one.

It may be hard to visualize how this interaction plays out in our heads, but this happens all day, every day. Once you understand the interworkings of our limbic system and our neocortex, many mental illnesses become far easier to understand. When our brains form, as children, the limbic system forms first, followed by the neocortex. For many children, the neocortex forms more slowly than their peers; therefore, when compared to other children in their class, the child has a hard time controlling his or her behavior. When they are less able to control themselves in a classroom setting, they are diagnosed with ADHD. It is as if the child has a little puppy in their head who wants to play and the child has not yet developed the executive functioning to train that puppy to be calm during class; therefore, the puppy is bouncing around from one distraction to another. If you have ever wondered why giving a child amphetamines (speed) makes them behave, it is because the amphetamines speed up the underdeveloped neocortex so that it can better control the child's behavior.

This is how our brains really work. We have a logical brain called the neocortex. This brain knows the rules (knows what is right and wrong). This is the brain that sets the alarm and gets us to work on time. It is the brain that weighs consequences of actions and inactions. The yin to the yang of the neocortex is the emotional center of the brain which is housed in the limbic system. All our interactions in our daily lives are a result of the conflict and negotiations that occur between the neocortex and the limbic system. For us to understand why we feel the way we do, we need to understand why we were made the way we were. My theory on how we were made is simple: God took the best parts of reptiles and mammals and paired them with our neocortex and made humans—simple as that. God took a mammal, added logic and reasoning to it, and—poof!—humans were made. Unfortunately, all the "animal" parts that kept us alive when we had to struggle to survive are now, in ways, problematic.

This was a great design thousands of years ago when food ran from us, but in the twenty-first century, this design caused some significant problems, problems we call mental illness. The technical term for this is cognitive dissonance—cognitive meaning thinking, and dissonance meaning lack of harmony. Cognitive dissonance is the state of having inconsistent thoughts or attitudes relating to behavioral decisions. This is a good definition of what would happen if you have two brains living in one skull, especially if one brain is emotionally driven and the other is intellectually driven.

I am, by no means, saying that all mental illness is caused by the disharmony between the neocortex and the limbic system, but that a good portion of depression, anxiety, addiction, and even PTSD is caused by this dissonance. Let's look at a few examples.

A married man works late one night. For this illustration, we will call his thinking brain Tom (his neocortex), and we will call his emotional brain Eric (his limbic system). Tom is a married man, he knows right from wrong, and he knows that being unfaithful to his wife is the wrong thing to do. Tom is unwavering in this fact because his Tom is purely logical. On one occasion, a young lady in the office looks at him seductively. For weeks, they had been exchanging looks and a few suggestive emails, but this is the first time they had been at the office alone after hours. Like the child in riding in the car with his father, Eric has just seen a sign that he cannot resist. Tom immediately tries to silence Eric, but as time goes on, the battle gets more intense. Tom begins to list all the reasons why this is a very bad idea. He makes very compelling arguments: he and Eric could lose their job, they could lose their wife, they could lose both. If someone found out, they would not only lose their job but their reputation and their career! Tom asks Eric, "What kind of idiot would do this?"

About this time, his heart starts racing because his brain stem, the primal part of his brain, just got the message that there is a conflict. There is also excitement because of the possibility of a sexual encounter, but that excitement is tempered with the realization that he could lose everything if he acts on his desires. As the minutes tick by, the conflict between Tom and Eric is beginning to intensify. Eric has begun flooding the body with chemicals to tip the scale in his favor. Just a few minutes earlier, Tom was rationalizing reasons not to accept the proposal, but now, as Eric begins to scale up the attack, Tom's resolve weakens. Eric starts saying things to Tom like "We may never get an opportunity like this again," or "She has as much to lose as I do, so no one will ever know."

On this occasion, Tom is faithful to his wife. However, this night becomes a tipping point. Tom and Eric realize they have feelings for this co-worker. Tom has decided that he is not going to be unfaithful to his wife, but Eric has decided that he is in love with their co-worker. For the next few months, the battle rages. Tom is trying to force Eric to let go of his feelings and honor his promise to his wife. Eric is working equally hard to get Tom to "follow his heart" and leave his wife. As the weeks go by, Tom becomes more depressed about his situation and anxious about what decision to make. Should he follow his head or his heart? His neocortex or his limbic system. Tom and Eric eventually end up in a counselor's office. To further illustrate this concept, consider these additional examples:

Example 1. A woman is sexually harassed at work.

Neocortex:	I cannot quit this job; I need to feed my children.
Limbic System:	This man frightens me and I may be sexually assaulted.
Result:	Her neocortex will tell her she must stay at the job she is in so she can support her family, but her limbic system will be afraid to go to work each day. Over time, the struggle between these two will lead to depression and anxiety.

Example 2. A family has no money for food

Neocortex:	We need food to survive; we should go to a food bank.
Limbic System:	I don't want them to know how poor we are.
Result:	Over time, the stress of trying to provide food and trying to keep it a secret will take a toll on both the parents and the children.

Example 3. A soldier returns from war.

Neocortex:	I am home; there is no danger.
Limbic System:	I have lived in danger for the past nine months; I know nothing else.
Result:	The longer the symptoms persist, the more likely depression will be the result. The soldier feels that since he is home, he "should" not feel the way he does. His neocortex knows he is no longer in danger, but his limbic system is still on high alert.

Example 4. A man gets divorced.

Neocortex: I am single now.
Limbic System: I miss the comfort and security of being married.
Result: His neocortex knows the marriage has ended; however, his limbic system takes a long time to fall in love and at least as long for those feelings to subside.

Example 5. A man stays in a high stress, high status, high-paying job.

Neocortex: I need to make a lot of money.
Limbic System: I am tired and burned out, and I cannot go on much longer.
Result: "The rat race," "keeping up with the Joneses," and euphemisms such as this describe his situation. He has monthly bills and obligations that keep him in a high-stress job. He wants to do something to lower stress, but that means lower pay. Over time, this will result in anxiety and depression and, consequently, addiction or suicide for some.

Example 6. An employee observes unethical behavior at work.

Neocortex: This needs to be reported.
Limbic System: If they find out I reported it, there will be repercussions.
Result: The employee wants to tell the authorities about the unethical behavior, but her limbic system knows there will be repercussions. Her neocortex tells her to do what is "right," but her limbic system fears what will happen if she does. This cognitive dissonance will cause anxiety and, if left unresolved, depression.

These are all examples of how one brain can be in conflict with the other. More importantly, they show what prolonged exposure to an intracranial conflict can do to a person's mental health. There are countless other examples. In each of these situations, the person experiencing the dissonance needs to acknowledge where the source of these feelings and ideas come from and have a discussion and negotiation on how to remedy the situation. Only the person in the situation can answer that question, but by knowing that being "of two minds" is not just a colloquialism; it is an important first step. The road to my recovery started when I removed the conflict between my neocortex and my limbic system and sat them down at a table in my head. Once Slick and I became friends and partners, my whole world changed.

My emotional break in 2009 was caused by a series of events like this. I had a series of challenges that caused a struggle inside my head for the right answer, and when I was unable to find one, I broke. After that, I had a series of additional challenges that culminated in my getting divorced. As you can imagine, from what I have stated so far, I was not a joy to live with. One evening I was walking Tahoe and I was feeling particularly lonely and down. Slick and I were blaming each other for our current situation; we were experiencing cognitive dissonance. He would say things like "Well, if you had been a stronger person, you'd still be married" or "You should have done a better job of communicating," to which I would reply, "Well, if you weren't so sensitive, we could have worked it out." There were several instances that Slick pointed out that I was to blame for the divorce, and he was upset, as was I. It was then that a very large light went on in my head. Slick was mad at me. Think about that for a moment. Slick, who is a physically distinct entity from my intellectual consciousness was angry at me . . . so I treated him accordingly. I treated Slick with the same dignity and respect that I would treat a roommate. I stopped my walk with Tahoe and told Slick out loud, "Slick, I'm sorry. I am truly sorry I was not a better husband to her. I am truly sorry that I was not a stronger man when I needed to be. I take responsibility for the situation we are in, and if you will give me a chance, I will make things better." What I did next is *crucial*, I asked Slick to forgive me. I said, "Slick, please forgive me and give me a chance to make it better."

What had happened that night is that I realized the human part of my brain, the neocortex, and the mammal part of my brain, the limbic system, had distinct personalities. Most people have heard of the conscious and subconscious and have a good idea of how they work. What we are taught from childhood though the remainder of our lives is to suppress our desires, to suppress our urges, and to essentially beat down that part of us that feels. That's what I had done, Slick was the part of me that had feelings . . . he was my feelings, and I did not give him a voice. I, like most people, tried to "get over it" or I tried to "beat myself up" for the divorce, well, I wasn't beating myself up, my neocortex (Jim) was beating up my limbic brain (Slick.) Jesus said it very well in Mark 3:25, "If a house is divided against itself it cannot stand." Our brains are not comprised of one consciousness but two distinct and equal entities that have to coexist inside our skulls. Up to this point, my neocortex had been dictating the terms of my existence and Slick had finally gotten burned out.

To illustrate these differences, I will use the game of charades as an example. The point of the game is to explain to a group of people a concept or idea without using words or any language in under a minute. Trying to explain to someone what a cat is only through the use of your hands is harder than it sounds. The reason the game is so much fun to watch is that it is so confusing to try to convey an idea, a bit of knowledge, to another human being without using language. It is actually pretty hilarious to watch someone jump about and become increasingly frustrated as the time expires. Ideas almost require some language to be communicated from one person to another.

Try this experiment: without language or writing, try to think of how you would teach something as simple as 2 + 2 = 4. You could use four match sticks and set them side by side and illustrate that there are four of them, but how would you explain the concept of math without talking? All you might really convey is that you could light four small fires. Our human brain needs language to communicate. Language is communication between neocortex and neocortex. Language is used to transfer knowledge from one person to another.

Conversely, Tahoe and I have spent countless hours together, never saying a word. Tahoe and I communicate limbic system to limbic system, feelings to feelings, emotion to emotion. I can say "bad dog" in a very happy voice, and then give him a treat and he will want me to say bad dog again; words mean nothing to him, it is my energy and emotion that he reads. We communicate very effectively without talking. I know when he's excited, or mad, or happy, or frustrated, and he reads my feelings better than any human can. I can read his emotions as easily as you are reading this book . . . but more importantly, he can read mine. I think that's why people love animals so much; it is because we talk with humans all day and sometimes we just need the feeling part of our brains to communicate without the clutter of language. Our neocortex is our logic center and our limbic system is our emotional center, and, oftentimes, they do not agree. When they do not agree, mental illness is likely to follow.

The fight and subsequent reconciliation and revelation that Slick and I had was exactly like a dispute between two roommates. What I realized was that I was not alone in my head, Slick and I were occupying the same space and we had to get along, because not getting along almost killed us. When I was in college, I had three roommates. When you live with a group of people for an extended period of time, there is going to be conflict. The caveat with roommates is that if you get angry with each other, you cannot simply part friends, never see each other again; when you are roommates, you have to work out the situation because you have a lease. You have many options as to working out disputes, but I can tell you, from many years of having roommates, the longer you are angry with each other, the worse the situation gets. In the house we shared, we had one roommate who would always buy food for himself and he would label it with his name. On more than one occasion, the rest of us would be hungry and perhaps had too much to drink. In our compromised state, we would often eat his food without permission. We knew it was his food, we knew it was wrong, and we did it anyway. When we were confronted with our crimes, all we could do was confess and ask for forgiveness.

This is how I treated Slick. I treated him as a roommate whom I had wronged. Now, had I wronged Slick? Honestly, it is irrelevant; what was important is that he felt that I had wronged him by allowing the divorce to occur. He felt I had at least partial culpability in the divorce, and since he was my roommate, I was responsible for us living alone again, which neither of us wanted. However, when I acknowledged how he felt, and more importantly, apologized to him for our being in the situation we were in, he forgave me and we continued our walk. As we walked, we talked about how living alone isn't so bad. We watched Tahoe check out all his normal spots, we looked at the moon, we had a nice walk. What I discovered that night is that a large portion of my depression and anxiety, if not all, emanated from miscommunication and unresolved struggles between Slick and me, or just to make sure I don't sound schizophrenic (too late right?), my neocortex and my limbic system.

What is important to understand is that there is a child in your head: a set of components in your brain have the sole job of producing emotions, the part science calls the limbic system. This is the part of the brain that is dominant when we are children and is still there and functioning as designed when we are adults. When we are ages one to four years old, our limbic system is our brain; we possess almost no cognitive ability. As we get older, that ability begins to grow as our neocortex grows. The neocortex does not replace the limbic system but grows on top of it. The child that is our limbic system is still there and never goes away. Some even believe it remains into our old age; when our neocortex fades, and we revert to a childhood state.

The limbic system is essentially in charge of our thoughts and feelings until we hit adolescence. As we move into our teens and our early twenties, the neocortex grows until it matures. Once the neocortex has matured, we have an "adult" brain. However, the adult brain did not replace the child brain; it merely was added to it. I believe that many of our decisions, addictions, and mental illnesses are the result of the balance or imbalance between the limbic system and the neocortex. If someone has an over active neocortex (as compared to the rest of the population) they will be seen as unemotional. Perhaps they may even be diagnosed with Asperger's. Conversely, if someone has an overactive limbic system, as compared to their neocortex, they will most likely be diagnosed with ADHD. There are two fantastic books on this subject. One is *Meet Your Happy Chemicals* by Loretta Graziano Breuning. The other is *On Intelligence* by Jeff Hawkins. I highly recommend that if you are reading this book, you read those two as well.

That child living in your head can be sad, or angry, or scared, and that anger or sadness is very real. When we hear phrases like "irrational fear," or "You're being silly," or "It's all in your head," those statements discount what is genuine. Who cares if the fear is irrational; that child in your head is afraid, and ignoring it or trying to suppress it will not make it stop. You need to acknowledge the scared, angry, sad child in your head and deal with it as you would with a child. If that child is scared, you need to acknowledge and reassure him or her that everything will be okay. If that child is sad, you need to comfort him or her and validate that sadness and allow it to happen, allow that child to be sad. If that child is angry, the rules are a little different. Normally, if a child is angry, the adult has to be the adult, but since this particular child is also an equal partner in the adult brain, you need to treat the angry child as an angry adult and negotiate a solution. That's what I had to do with Slick on more than one occasion, and as crazy as it may sound, it works. It "got me to midnight" on more than one occasion and saved my life.

Let's take a moment and go through an exercise that explains what I am talking about. Tina is a thirty-eight-year-old professional who lives in Chicago. In this exercise, we will call Tina's neocortex Tina and her limbic brain will be called Erica. It is very important to give names to both these entities as they are distinct and need to be treated as such. It is 4:00 PM on a Thursday, when her boss walks in and informs her that today is the last day at her job; due to budget cuts, her position has been eliminated. Tina and Erica both are panicked by this news. Who will pay the mortgage and car payment and all the other bills? She has some savings, but not much. How much will her severance be, if she even receives one? How long can she be without a job? Is her resume updated and complete? She spends a few minutes with her thoughts racing. After about five minutes of thoughts and fear, she takes a deep breath and composes herself. It is at this point when something *very* important happens. She composes herself. *Tina* composes herself . . . Erica is still freaking out! Please understand this part; Tina, the neocortex, is composed and ready to take on the task of finding a new job and moving forward. Tina, the logical side, has processed the information and has formulated a plan of action. Erica, the limbic system has not! Erica is still in panic mode, and will be, for some time. The reason that this is so crucial is that Tina will "beat herself up" for not getting over it. Tina will become frustrated by the fact that "she" is still upset. This is because Tina does not know Erica exists. Tina believes, like most of us, that she has one brain and that she should be able to control it. This frustration will culminate with Tina getting mad at Erica for not calming down. The angrier Tina gets, the more upset and scared Erica gets.

As days and weeks go by, Tina is doing all she can to find a new job. She is applying for jobs, networking with her friends, and searching the internet for new positions, she is working her plan. Tina has made "finding a job" her new job. However, because Tina does not see Erica as a separate entity, she is still trying to force Erica to comply, relax, and calm down. She asks herself "I know I will find a job. Why am I still so scared?" Tina then gets angry with herself and is frustrated because she cannot get over being afraid. What she does not realize is that she, Tina, is fine, but it is the part of her brain, the limbic system, the emotional center of the brain, where Erica lives, that is scared.

What if Tina took a moment and said to Erica, "I know you're scared. I am, too, but we will get through this." By acknowledging Erica's feelings (which are really her feelings) and saying that things will get better, and they are doing all they can to make that happen, the situation has not changed. Tina and Erica's perception of the situation has changed. Erica is afraid of the unknowns, just like a child who is going to the dentist for the first time. Once Tina acknowledges and *validates* Erica's feelings, which again are her own feelings, her situation improves. I have used this technique countless times and it has been very successful. Remember, if you can beat yourself up, you can calm yourself down. Have you ever done something you regret and yelled at yourself, "How could you be so stupid?!" or "You went and did it again!" Who exactly are you talking to? Why do we only do that in negative situations? Why not try the reverse? If you beat yourself up for failures, lift yourself up for successes.

In order to calm yourself down, or cheer yourself up, or talk yourself off the ledge, you need to know who your "self" is. Your "self" is two equal components: your thinking brain and your feeling brain—your thoughts and your feelings, your mind and soul, your spirit and your flesh.

In counseling, there are numerous techniques used to calm down a client. One of the most common techniques is to have the client breathe slowly and deeply from the diaphragm. The theory and science behind the technique is to attempt to create a feedback loop to tell the limbic system to calm down. When a person gets anxious, breathing becomes shallow, heart rate increases, and non-essential systems, such as digestion, slow down in an effort to prepare the body to fight or flee. Essentially, the limbic system is in a state of anxiety. It feels that something bad is about to happen, and we need to prepare for it. We are unable to voluntarily control our heart rate or our digestion; however, we can control the rate of our breathing and the type of breathing we do. By telling a client to breathe deeply from the diaphragm, we are attempting to send a message to the limbic system that there is no reason to be afraid and the hope is that the components will receive the message and begin to slow the heart rate and return to a resting state. What I would counsel Tina to do is to sit quietly, breathe deeply, and have a conversation with Erica, her limbic system. I would instruct her to do the breathing technique, but I would also instruct her to open an actual dialogue between her neocortex and the part of her brain that is in distress, Erica. In my experience, this has been a very successful technique.

Let's take the example of PTSD. Jake Davis is a fictional twenty-one-year-old man who is a corporal in the United States Army. Jake is an average man with an uneventful upbringing. He joined the army to protect his country and to help pay for college. After completing basic training, Jake is sent to a foreign country to help the army protect America's interests abroad. While on patrol one day, Jake hears a dog start barking. A few moments later, the vehicle he is in is hit with a high-powered explosive. The vehicle is launched several feet into the air and lands on its side. Jake is injured in the blast, but not severely. He is stunned but gains his composure. When he realizes what happened, he finds himself in an immobilized vehicle with enemy soldiers shooting at him. A protracted firefight ensues and several of the members of Jake's team are killed. Jake is in the midst of a real fight-or-flight scenario where he could likely be killed. In the heat of the battle, every component of Jake's limbic system that was built to keep him alive is operating exactly as it was designed. His adrenal system is pumping out adrenaline to keep him at full alert, heightening all his senses. His heart is pounding to ensure that he has adequate oxygenated blood to all his muscles to prepare and participate in the battle.

In this moment of chaos, his neocortex is essentially along for the ride. The functions of his thinking brain will hinder him, as he needs to react to the immediate danger. Thinking about what is happening in this moment could easily cause hesitation and could get him and his team killed. For example, if Jake's thinking brain says, "Let me take a moment and evaluate my choices here. I can shoot back, I can find a better hiding place, I can try to negotiate with the people shooting at me, I mean they never met me, I could show them what a nice guy I am and that I'm just here to keep the peace. Who doesn't want peace right? Is this a just war? What if I kill one of these people shooting at me? Can I live with that? How old are these people shooting at me? Oh man, what if I shoot a kid?" If Jake took a few moments to think like this, he would likely be killed, as the danger was immediate and real. When I say our limbic system is designed to keep us alive, this is the type of scenario I am referring to.

After what seems like an eternity, help arrives. Additional soldiers and equipment arrive to assist Jake and his team. When the dust settles, Jake and the other survivors of the battle are taken back to the base to receive medical treatment. Jake's deployment continues for another seven months. While there are no more incidents such as this for the remainder of his tour of duty, Jake's limbic system remains on high alert for the duration of his time there. He continues to do daily patrols ever vigilant and always scanning the landscape for potential danger. Every time he climbs into his patrol vehicle, his heart begins to race, his muscles tense, and his senses are heightened. Finally, after seven months, Jake is on a plane home. Upon arriving at home, Jake is greeted by his family and friends. They go to his parents' house and have a wonderful party for him . . . he is home.

The following morning, Jake and his parents are driving to the store to pick up some groceries. While they are driving, they are talking about what his plans are for his career in the army. As the car approaches a stop sign, a dog begins barking. Jake's limbic system immediately springs into high alert. While his neocortex knows that he is in his parents' car and there is no danger, his limbic system knows that the last time he was in a vehicle and a dog barked, an explosion and firefight immediately followed. His adrenal system is pumping out adrenaline to keep him at full alert; it heightens all his senses. His heart is pounding to ensure that he has adequate oxygen to all his muscles to prepare and participate in the battle . . . except he's at a stop sign in his hometown half a world away from the war he just left. Jake has PTSD.

This is where I part ways with the mental health community, because, in my opinion, Jake does not have a disorder; his brain is doing exactly what it was designed to do. One week prior, when Jake was still in the warzone, if he had heard that dog barking, his limbic system triggering into high alert would have saved his life; but this week, Jake is home, and his limbic system still thinks that danger is present. This will likely be the case for the rest of his life. Jake's thinking brain knows where he is, he knows cognitively he is home, and the war is in a distant country, but his emotional brain has been trained that a dog barking signals danger and he needs to prepare for it.

In this scenario, it is easy to see how Jake ended up in this situation. He was in constant danger for several months and now he is not. His limbic system was in charge for the duration of his deployment to keep him safe from the dangers of war, but now that the danger is no longer present, his limbic system needs time to internalize the fact that the danger is gone. This is where the neocortex has to carry the load. What if rather than tell Jake that he has a disorder, we have Jake acknowledge that he has two components in his brain, his neocortex and his limbic system . . . his thinking brain and his emotional brain. What if we had Jake name his limbic system "Corporal Davis," and rather than fight against Corporal Davis, we had Jake talk to him and say something like "Corporal, thank you for keeping us alive. Thank you for staying on alert for all those months. You did an incredible job and I'm proud to share a life with you. Thank you, soldier, for your service. Now it's time to rest."

We see this phenomenon in animals, so being that our limbic system is the same as theirs, we should not be surprised that we behave similarly. I used to have a dog named Ted. Ted was one of the coolest dogs ever; I was blessed to have eleven years with him. However, Ted hated kids. *Hated* kids. At some point in his life, prior to our getting together, a child did something to him that imprinted on his limbic system: kids were evil and needed to be bitten. No matter how I tried to break this conditioning, Ted would growl and try to snap at anyone under four feet tall. Could we say that Ted had PTSD? Sure, but we do not ascribe PTSD to dogs. Why not, the formula is the same. The reason we do not is because humans have a highly developed neocortex and we "should" be able to get over it. PTSD is a disorder because it is a disharmony between our neocortex and our limbic system. Since Ted did not have a human neocortex, there was no disharmony, Ted hated kids and he was completely fine with that. PTSD is only a disorder if the environment is not a dangerous one. In a war zone, PTSD is an asset. This is why so many soldiers want to return to combat when they get home. Their disorder is only a disorder when the danger is gone. Where there is danger, their neocortex and limbic system find harmony. The neocortex sees the danger and their limbic system responds.

Hopefully, this illustration demonstrates how the limbic system will adapt in times of crisis to keep us alive. Many of us who never went to war or never were in a situation like Jake's, struggle with traumatic experiences that have left their mark on our lives. Then there are some of us who were born with the disorders that present themselves as anxiety or depression or both. The primary difference between PTSD and an anxiety disorder is that with PTSD, we have knowledge of the cause. Having panic attack symptoms because a dog barking reminds you of a time when your life was in danger and having a panic attack because it's two thirty in the afternoon, and your brain just decides to panic, leads to the same result . . . a panic attack. While in the midst of my depression and anxiety attacks, I did not know what was going on, but after years of research, I have a good idea. While I am not a scientist and none of my degrees are in neurology, I have what I would consider a functional understanding of the systems in our brains that make us who we are. In the next chapter, I am going to attempt to share my knowledge of how it all works, and what happens when it does not work out the way we hoped it would.

Having a direct conversation with the limbic system is not just a theory for me. Recently, I was informed that the company I work for was sold, and my position was being eliminated. In two weeks, I will be without a job. Upon hearing this news, I was understandably upset. I got very nervous, but I practiced the techniques above. I breathed deeply and had a long talk with Slick. We walked Tahoe and planned for what was ahead. I updated my resume and began the search for a new job. I was concerned, but appropriately concerned. I, a man with an anxiety disorder, major depression, and ADHD, was fine. I was fine because Slick and I had a talk, and we looked for another job, and one came. I addressed the two sides of my brain. The thinking side had a plan. The feeling side had been acknowledged and validated. We were fine. This technique works.

CHAPTER 8

Denning's Uncertainty Principle

"Life is strong and fragile. It's a paradox . . . It's both
things, like quantum physics: It's a particle and a
wave at the same time. It all exists all together."
—Joan Jett

HEISENBERG'S UNCERTAINTY PRINCIPLE simply states
that the position of an object and the speed of an object cannot be
accurately measured at the same time. For example, if you are in a car
racing down the highway at 150 miles per hour and a friend calls you
and asks where you are, and you reply "we are at mile marker 74," by
the time you reply you have passed mile marker 74. The more accurately you are able to measure the position of an object, the less accurately you can measure the velocity of the object and vice-versa. The
same was becoming true with my exploration into how my mind
worked. When I was trying to figure out who was really in charge of
my actions, the task became exceedingly difficult. In some situations,
my limbic system was in charge, and in other situations, it was my
neocortex. What I was sure of was that as long as I assumed that I had
one brain I had no chance of accurately understanding how any of it
worked. The more closely I measured my thinking brain's behavior,
the less accurately I could measure my feeling brain. The more logis-
tical I became, the less emotional I became, and conversely, the more
emotional I became, the less rational I became. When I realized that

our brains are not one object that is both emotional and logical, but two separate entities, one that is emotional and one that is logical, things made much more sense to me.

Have you ever seen a person whom you are romantically interested in and would like to talk to, but for fear of rejection you walked away? The Yaghan language (indigenous language of Tierra del Fuego) has a word that I'm not going to try to pronounce; it is Mamihlapinatapai. Loosely translated, it is the act of two people who are interested in one another, but out of fear, choose not to engage. This word is listed in the Guinness Book of World Records as the "most succinct word." It is also a very succinct example of how our brains work. A person's neocortex can see a beautiful woman sitting alone and say, "Hey, I should go talk to her," but their emotional brain will kick in and say, "She's too pretty for you" or "She probably has a boyfriend" or any of a thousand reasons why he shouldn't talk to her. This is a scenario where fear and emotion will trump logic. Logic says, "She is alone and the only way to find out if she's single is to ask," but emotion and fear will stop it from happening. In this situation, the limbic system stopped you from acting.

In a totally different circumstance, perhaps a supervisor will say something in an emotional outburst like "I cannot believe how stupid you are!" After hearing this attack, the emotional brain will want to punch the supervisor in the throat! However, the neocortex will do a cost benefit analysis and say, "If you punch him in the throat we will be unemployed, sent to jail, and will not be able to get another job. So don't do it." Again, this is a situation where the two brains are in conflict and must negotiate a solution.

We've been told that in scenarios like this, the behavior we choose is based on the interaction between the conscious and subconscious, but I disagree, as both components have equal input as to what the outcome will be, given the scenario. In my situation, when I was in the depths of my depression, my Slick was not healthy . . . not even close. I realized that until he was healthy, I (Jim) had to pick up the slack. The Denning Uncertainty Principle is my way of describing the struggle I face in making those decisions. Every time Slick whispered in my ear that I should kill myself, I had a decision to make. Until I gave Slick a voice, it was a one-sided decision. I had always believed I had a conscience and a subconscience, but this is not correct; I have an emotional conscience and a logical conscience, and they are equal. Slick never wanted to die; he just wanted me to listen, and when I wouldn't, he wanted to kill me. He wanted to die and that required both of us to die. Now that I listen, we get along a *lot* better . . . obviously.

Science tells us that the neocortex "influences" the limbic system, which is true, but the opposite is true too, the limbic system influences the neocortex as well. In mental health counseling, we are told that sheer force of will is what we need to overcome suicidal ideation or addiction. I disagree; I believe that once we understand that our brain is comprised of equal components, and we have a talk with both sides and make decisions as a partnership, overcoming adversity becomes much easier. On those lonely nights when I was contemplating suicide, I was trying to forcibly suppress Slick, and Slick was forcibly trying to kill me. The battle was in my head, not the real world. The negotiation I had with Slick was just to give me one more day, let me "make it to midnight" and tomorrow we would try again. This was the Denning Uncertainty Principle; the two sides of my psyche were at war.

CHAPTER 9

Anakin Skywalker and Darth Vader

"In a dark place we find ourselves, and a little
more knowledge lights our way."
—Yoda

ONE OF THE greatest pop culture examples of the limbic system phenomenon is the story of Anakin Skywalker and Darth Vader. When Anakin was a young man, he was very much like most of us— wanted to do what was right. In the first episode of the Star Wars saga, Anakin was portrayed as a very intelligent young man, and a talented engineer. He had a good head on his shoulders and had excellent teachers that provided a foundation for him. Like Anakin, we are all essentially born with a clean slate. We are born into a world that is comprised of both good and evil. Some people are born into immediate surroundings that are not as conducive to the development of this slate as others who are born into surroundings that are both nurturing and supportive. Relating this to Anakin's story, it is apparent that his limbic system becomes more and more prominent in his thinking. As time goes on, Anakin's strong-willed nature and mistrust of authority become more obvious. Like Anakin, as we enter adolescence and begin our journey in to adulthood, we are presented with opportunities to "follow the ways of The Force," i.e., to do what is right in the eyes of the world, or to embrace the Dark Side.

What Star Wars gives us is a concrete example of the players in this saga that we experience every day. Obi-Wan Kenobi represents the example for Anakin to follow in his quest to become a Jedi. He is a solid teacher and has Anakin's best interests at heart, as well as what is best for the Jedi order. Obi-Wan Kenobi can be compared to mentors, pastors, teachers, and professors in our lives. These are the people who wish for us to succeed in life and reach our fullest potential for both ourselves and society as a whole. Like the patrons at Studebakers who attempted to guide me down the path of not smoking, drinking, or doing drugs, Obi-Wan Kenobi was trying to guide Anakin down the path of righteousness. As the story unfolds, circumstances arise that cause Anakin to make decisions predominantly from his emotional brain instead of his thinking brain. Recognizing this, Obi-Wan Kenobi gives him the following advice, "Be mindful of your thoughts, Anakin. They'll betray you." Again, if we have but one brain, how can *our* thought betray *us*? They cannot, but our feeling brain can very easily betray our thinking brain. And in moments of vulnerability, the Dark Side, or in our world, dark forces can seize on those moments and capitalize on them.

This is what we see happen to Anakin. In a moment of rage, Anakin uses his Jedi skills, skills meant to serve The Force, to slaughter an entire community of Sand People who had kidnapped and murdered his mother. It was in this moment of emotional upheaval that the emperor seized on the opportunity to co-opt Anakin to the Dark Side. While I would not expect Anakin not to lash out at the people who killed his mother, it provides us a clear picture of what can happen to us, and everyone around us, when we allow our emotional brain to take control. One moment of passion, one decision to drive when we shouldn't, one experiment with a gateway drug, can open the door to a future, that, like Anakin, leads to destruction.

People who, like me, have a diagnosed mental illness have a much more difficult time resisting the temptation of the Dark Side. I cannot count the hours, days, weeks, and months of struggle and misery that I endured because I did not understand what was happening. I remember many times, after a long day at work, trying to maintain my composure and pretending that everything was fine, I would be exhausted and vulnerable to the attacks of temptation. As soon as I got to the parking lot, I would get into my car and either bang my head on the steering wheel or literally punch myself in the head in an attempt to make the pain stop. I knew I was in pain, emotional pain, which is, in many cases, worse than physical pain, but I did not know why. Once I realized that I had an emotional brain, and it was, for reasons unknown to me, rebelling against me, I was able to better address the problem. While I was not able to fix it, just the understanding of the issue helped me in handling it more effectively.

The best parallel I can refer to, once again, is an automotive analogy. Years ago, I had a car that I had replaced the engine in. It was a 1968 Plymouth Fury. She was a five-thousand-pound epic masterpiece of the artisans who ruled Detroit in the sixties. This was before the internet, so replacing an engine was, in many cases, trial and error. One day, I was driving down a back road, testing my work to see how the car ran. Much to my surprise, I had neglected to put a spring on the carburetor, which turned out to be a very important spring. This spring closed the flow of air and gas to the carburetor when I took my foot off the gas pedal. It was late at night when I stepped on the gas of a five-thousand-pound car equipped with one of the biggest engines the sixties muscle car era had to offer. When I took my foot off the pedal, I realized I was now merely a passenger in a rapidly accelerating five-thousand-pound projectile. Being me, I had replaced the engine before replacing the brakes, so the brakes were essentially useless at this point. After a moment of panic, and getting right with the Lord, I reached for the key and turned off the engine and coasted safely to a stop.

When someone is severely depressed or has a panic attack, this is essentially what happens. There is a flood of chemicals that will result in experiencing emotional pain, or in the case of a panic attack, paralyzing fear, with no discernible cause. This is the hell that is mental illness. Like the aptly named 1968 Plymouth Fury that I was driving with a wide open throttle, the brain of someone with depression or anxiety has a wide open throttle of misery. Unlike my problem with my car, there is no off switch in the limbic system. This is the essence of my uncertainty principle. I was not only uncertain about when this would happen, but I was also uncertain about the decisions I would make when I was in this state. When the emotional pain is excruciating, you will do almost anything to make it stop. When a person hits the point that they will do *anything* to make the pain stop, anything can rapidly turn into a decision that cannot be undone. Anything can become an ill-advised sexual encounter, or a drinking binge, or even a full-blown drug induced bender… and for some, suicide.

CHAPTER 10

Medication

"The greatest medicine of all is teaching people
how not to need it."
—Hippocrates

IF YOU ARE reading this, there is a better-than-average chance that, at some point, you might have been on an antidepressant. If you have ever been on an antidepressant and have had to discontinue its use, you can relate to this. I was first put on an antidepressant when I was twenty-three years old. I was told, "Hey, Jim . . . take this and you'll feel better," and actually, that is what happened. I took Paxil, and after a while I began to feel better. Paxil is in the class of drugs called a Selective Serotonin Reuptake Inhibitor or SSRI. These drugs effectively increase the amount of serotonin in the brain, which helps with depression, anxiety, and numerous other ailments. These drugs do a fantastic job, but for most people, these drugs are meant to be utilized short-term. In the road trip scenario, Lucas was excited about seeing the animals, similarly, our limbic system is excited about SSRIs. These pills make "us" feel good, which really translates into "it makes our limbic system feel good." Now, if we follow the logic from the car ride, what happens if we take those SSRI's away from the limbic system? As you would expect, there will be a tantrum.

A couple of years after I started taking Paxil, my doctor and I agreed that I should stop taking them as my life situation had improved substantially. This is a big disclaimer . . . do *not* stop taking medication without talking to your doctor first; I made that mistake and regretted it. My doctor and I had agreed that I would cease taking the Paxil, which I did. On the first day, it was no big deal. I felt fine, and life was good. However, on the second day, Slick was starting to notice that I had not taken my Paxil for over twenty-four hours, and he was becoming agitated. At this point in my life, I was not aware of Slick or my limbic system or what "withdrawal" was, so I was becoming increasingly confused about how I felt and what was going on in my head. All I knew was that my mood was shifting rapidly, and I was becoming increasingly uncomfortable.

By the third day, I was starting to experience what are referred to as "brain zaps." These are a common side effect of discontinuing a SSRI too quickly. It felt like an electrical zap whenever I would move my eyes to the left or right. In addition to the brain zaps, I was experiencing severe stomach cramps, along with dizziness and an inability to think. I remember thinking to myself that this was worse than the symptoms I had experienced before taking the medication! For a while, I believed that I had broken my brain, and that the medication I had taken had changed my brain chemistry to such an extent that I was going to be taking this medication for the rest of my life. Fortunately, Slick acclimated to my discontinuation of the medication over time, but it was brutal.

For the next fifteen years I was on and off SSRIs as my life situation changed. When I was depressed, I would go on a new SSRI, and when the depression subsided, I would get off them. In 2009, upon having, for lack of a better word, a "nervous breakdown" I again sought the assistance of a psychiatrist. Now, at this point, let me throw out a *huge* disclaimer. Pharmaceuticals are extremely helpful to a great many people; I am just not one of them. So please do not interpret what I am going to say as a condemnation of pharmaceutical remedies for mental disorders; it is most assuredly not . . . it is just a recap of my experience. The best course of action is to always seek the help of a professional physician, counselor, psychologist, or other mental health professional . . . preferably all the above. I visited eleven doctors, counselors, and other mental health and medical professionals before I finally found what worked for me. So please do not discount the help of professionals, seek them diligently as if your life depends on it . . . because it does.

One recommendation I will make, with the caveat that this was just my experience, is to find the person who has graduated most recently in their respected field. I have found their knowledge is the most recent and they are more familiar with what is the current best practice. Also, someone who is new in the field is more likely to seek the help of someone more experienced. I have found that experienced medical professionals are less likely to seek the counsel of others. When I first started my journey, I sought out the most experienced doctors. While they were well intentioned, they had been doing what they were taught decades ago. It was not until I found young medical professionals that I learned about the advancements in treatments and supplements that are available, many available over the counter.

My second recommendation is to get to know your pharmacist. Should you be prescribed medication, your pharmacist can tell you what you can expect from these medications and the potential side effects. It is not an understatement to say my pharmacist saved my life. He took the time to explain to me what I could expect from taking different medications how taking different drugs back to back would actually be more harmful than staggering the dosages. On one occasion, I did not ask him about a new medication I was put on. The result was my attempting to stand up and immediately losing consciousness due to a steep drop in blood pressure. I awoke to paramedics standing in my bedroom at two o'clock in the morning. Fortunately, I had regained consciousness while they were there and did not need to take a ride. I found out later that the pills I had taken did not go well with the three beers I had consumed earlier. This was a potentially deadly combination. When I mentioned the incident to my pharmacist, he pointed at the sticker on the bottle and said, "Jim, which part of do not take with alcohol is unclear?" We had developed a good relationship at this point, so he felt comfortable in kindly telling me to read the dang labels! One thing I cannot stress enough is to read the pharmaceutical labels, *and* listen to the commercials. If you hear "may cause suicidal thoughts or actions" listen to them.

I have tachyphylaxis. Tachyphylaxis is the rapid decrease in the effectiveness of a drug soon after its administration. For people like me, a prescribed medication will no longer be effective after a few days or weeks. The problem is that when we try to get off the medication, we are generally worse off than when we started. For example, you might have chronic headaches and you are prescribed a pain medication that makes the headaches go away, but after taking it for a week, your headaches come back. Since the medicine is no longer working, you stop taking it. Within that week, your body has become acclimated to the medication so when you stop taking it your headaches come back, but now they are far worse than they were before.

Upon having my breakdown, I was prescribed a benzodiazepine medication called Klonopin. Klonopin was able to calm my anxiety for one day, maybe two, but by the third day, my body had acclimated to the medication, and I was just as miserable as I was before, but now I was on a medication that had no benefits. My psychiatrist suggested we increase the dosage, which we did. As expected, after a few more days, I was back to where I was, but I had twice as much medication coursing through my veins. This was my first introduction to addiction . . . in under two weeks, I was addicted to Klonopin.

When I attempted to stop Klonopin because I perceived it was not working, my situation deteriorated very quickly. My depression and anxiety immediately doubled from what it was prior to starting Klonopin, primarily because my brain had acclimated to the medication. Without it, I was going through withdrawals; this was when the thought of suicide popped into my head. In 2009, Stevie Nicks publicized the dangers of Klonopin by describing her own detox from the prescription drug as "hellish" and worse than withdrawing from cocaine or heroin.

For years, pharmaceuticals had made me feel better, but now the medications no longer worked, and they actually were making me worse. I remember this was when I became suicidal, I had lost hope. The rationale for the suicidal thoughts were, if I had a problem and the solution made the problem worse, that meant there was no solution. Over the next year, my psychiatrist tried numerous other medications for depression and anxiety, but the results were the same; either there was a worsening of my symptoms or, at best, no appreciable effects at all. After Klonopin failed, he switched me over to a series of Selective Serotonin Reuptake Inhibitors (SSRIs) such as Paxil, Prozac, Celexa, Lexapro, and others. The real problem with these drugs is that they take weeks to build up a "therapeutic dose." Those are weeks of utter despair and hopelessness. When the requisite time has passed, and there is no relief, the hopelessness is compounded. Unfortunately, the answer I got when it came time to see the doctor was "Let's increase the dosage," which was the same answer my doctor gave his patients when he graduated in 1976. Unfortunately, for many, this is still the answer.

For the next five years, I bounced from one medication to another, and one doctor to another, praying that the next doctor would have the answer. I went from one psychiatrist to another, hoping to find some relief, but unfortunately, my physiology does not do well with medication. The years of taking SSRIs essentially made me immune to them. I then went to a neurologist, an endocrinologist, and a general practitioner. I met with counselors and even an allergy specialist, but to no avail.

At some point on my journey, I heard a commercial for one of the medications I was taking and that little disclaimer line that is in so many commercials for different pharmaceuticals seemed to scream out at me, "This medication may cause suicidal thoughts or actions." Well in my case, it did. I remember sitting on the couch and thinking, "Well, how awesome is this? I'm suicidal and I am taking medications that cause suicidal thoughts or actions." Hope was very quickly fading as I was finding my options exhausted. This is a very dark and hopeless line of reasoning, but I learned that reasoning and mental illness are not compatible. Finally, the psychiatrist I was seeing said that my symptoms were treatment resistant. He was essentially saying that there were no pills that would help me. He suggested that I consider going on disability and not working any more. He and my counselor told me I needed to accept being suicidal and depressed as my "new normal."

It was then that I decided to change the way I thought. I made the decision that being suicidal was not an option; it was a symptom. I accepted the fact that, while all the mental health professionals I had visited were very capable and good at their professions, they were unable to help me. I was going to have to find my answers on my own. The doctors and counselors I visited had a vast array of tools, but their tools did not fit my situation. I needed to find my own tools. I needed to create a toolkit specifically for me. Some of the tools I had taken from them, some I found on my own, some came from the experiences of others . . . and the greatest tool came from God, through a methamphetamine-addicted prison inmate named Mike.

CHAPTER 11

The Toolkit

"When I let go of what I am, I become
what I might be."
—Lao Tzu

WITH THE HELP of this book, I not only want to write about what I did to beat depression, anxiety, and most importantly, being suicidal, but I also want to give you the tools to hopefully do the same. In order to do that, I need to explain what I did to change the way I thought about my brain, but what's more important, I want to change the way that you think about *your* brain. We have covered how our brains are divided into two primary components: I named mine Jim and Slick. Jim is the spirit, the neocortex, the rational side of my brain. Slick is the flesh, the limbic system and the emotional side of my brain. It was imperative for me to make peace with these two sides of my brain, not as an impartial observer but as a very involved participant. I guess I was fortunate enough to have an inquisitive mind from an early age, and phrases like "beat yourself up" and "talk yourself into it" made no sense to me until I realized that both parts of my brain had equal votes in each decision I made. Psychologists say we have a conscious and subconscious mind, but I disagree. I believe that I have two equal parts of my brain that occupy different components of my psyche. One is emotional and one is logical. The standard paradigm of counseling and psychology is to use the rational mind to essentially manipulate or force the emotional part to do the will of the rational part. I lost that fight many times, so instead of continuing to battle each other, both parts of my brain have developed a partnership. I have to tell you; I've never been happier or more at peace.

In counseling school, we learn to use tools like mindfulness. We learn to tell clients to focus on the now: focus on the trees, and the smells, and the sounds around us. This tool is useful, as it is designed to calm down that emotional side that is either depressed or anxious. I decided, instead of trying to trick my emotional side into being calm, I would just talk to it, like a "rational" human being. I say, "Hey, Slick, relax, man, we got this. Check out that cloud formation, isn't that cool?" If there's no clouds to look at when Slick is having a bad day, I'll ask him, "Hey, Slick, remember that time we went to the beach and watched the sun come up? Remember watching the pelicans soar just above the waves? Do you remember feeling the dampness of the morning air and the smell of the salt? Remember the sounds of the boats going out to sea? That was a great morning, wasn't it?" Then we will sit and reminisce about all the mornings we have spent watching the sun rise at the beach. These fond memories of mornings at Port Aransas have gotten me through some very tough times.

I still used all the counseling skills I had acquired, but I used them with full disclosure; I don't try to "fool myself" into compliance. I treat Slick with respect. I treat him as an equal, not a negative force that needs to be manipulated into submission. Hopefully, some of the tools I have used will prove helpful to you, as well.

Let me fully disclose at this point; I am a man with no children, and I am not married. I was married before. I have never served in the military. My solutions were tailored to my situation as a married man, and then a single man with no children and no military service. Having children, and/or a spouse has its own unique set of circumstances that creates its own unique set of challenges. Having served in the military also has its own unique set of circumstances that can manifest itself. My sincere hope and prayer is that some of this information will be of use to you in some shape or form.

"Make It to Midnight"

It may seem obvious that I would come out of the gate with this one; however, I have good reason. You have to make a decision—a decision to live and "make it stick." When I finally decided to quit smoking, it was not easy. For years, I had quit and relapsed; it happened more times than I can count. Finally, one day, I decided to quit quitting. I was done. I decided I was either going to smoke or I was going to quit smoking, but I was done. What I did not know at the time is that when Jim told Slick I was done . . . it stuck.

Fifteen years later, I did the same thing. I had a talk with Slick and said we were going to live and that was it. When this happened, we were not on friendly terms, but regardless, that is what happened, and again, it worked. If I can give you any bit of advice it is this: make the decision to *live*. If that seems too hard, just make the decision to "make it to midnight."

Tie a String

When I was a child (with ADHD) and my mom wanted me to remember something, she would tie a string around my finger. While I looked really silly with a string on my finger, her home remedy for forgetfulness worked. After I made the decision not to end my life, I needed a daily reminder of my decision. There were times when the days seemed exceptionally long and midnight seemed like an eternity away. I realized I needed something tangible to look at that would remind me of my pact with God that I was going to live.

For a while, I wore a watch set to military time. At any point in the day, I could look at the watch and see how many hours I had left to midnight. This actually worked really well. Other days I would set the countdown timer if I needed some extra help. Finally, I decided I needed something a little more permanent. Six hours later and $400 lighter, I had a beautiful tattoo on my right shoulder. It is a very ornate pocket watch set to midnight. At the bottom of the watch, I had the artist add the Bible verse Matthew 6:34: "Therefore do not worry about tomorrow, for tomorrow will worry about itself. Each day has enough trouble of its own."

I am *not* recommending getting a tattoo, but it worked. On the days when I was feeling like I did not want to go on, I pulled up my sleeve, looked up to heaven, and made it to midnight.

Tell Someone

A recent study by Johns Hopkins Bloomberg School of Public Health has shown that people who lose a loved one to suicide are at increased risk for a number of mental and physical disorders. These include cancer, depression, herniated discs, and mood disorders. According to the study leader, Annette Erlangsen, PhD, "It is an exceedingly devastating experience when someone you love dearly dies suddenly by suicide. We were able to show that being exposed to such a stressful life event as the suicide of your partner holds higher risks for physical and mental disorders and is different from losing a partner from other causes of death, such as illness or sudden accident" (https://medicalxpress.com/news/2017-03-spousal-suicide-affect-bereaved-spouse.html#nRlv).

I know that when I was contemplating suicide, I would think, "I'm such a burden, everyone would be better off without me." This is empirical and peer reviewed evidence that your loved ones will *not* be better off without you. Please, do it for them. The first time I told someone how I felt was on a weekend when I was playing guitar at church. We were praying before rehearsal and the worship leader asked, "Does anyone have any prayer requests?" I replied, "I do. I am suicidal and have been for a few years now, and I do not know what to do." You could have heard a pin drop. Then the pastor walked up and said, "What do you need?" That was the perfect answer. No one tried to fix it, no one offered advice, no one told me how great my life was, they just asked, "How can we help?"

Growing up, I was very careless, or carefree, depending on who was paying the medical bills. I rode my bike with no protection of any kind, and yet, I rode it like I was indestructible. I rode a skateboard the same way. I learned on numerous occasions that I am "destructible." Every time I would fall, the same thing happened instinctually. The part of my body that was injured would be pulled toward my chest and the rest of my body would fall in around it. When I broke my wrist, I pulled my wrist to my chest and put my other hand over it to cover it. When I broke my ankle, I sat down and wrapped my hands around it to protect it. The same thing happened at church that day. I, a member of that church body, was injured, and the rest of the church gathered around me to protect me.

Ironically, when the pastor asked, "What do you need?" I had no answer. I did not "need" anything from them; I just needed someone to *care*. I needed to stop pretending that I was okay. I needed to drop my mask and shield and say, "I am hurting and I need someone to know, I need someone to care."

The act of saying it out loud is life-changing. Find a person, a person who cares about you. Tell them that you may call them from time to time and say, "Talk me down, man!" Explain to them you just need to stop pretending for a few minutes. You need someone to say, "I'm sorry you're hurting." There were many times I would call my person and tell her, "I can't do this anymore. I really want it all to end." She would reply, "Do you need me to fix it or do you need me to listen?" I would reply, "No, I just needed to say it." We had that conversation many times, and sometimes that was the totality of the conversation. There was something about saying it out loud that caused it to sink in to Slick. Once I realized that saying how I felt out loud made such a huge difference, I did it when I was alone at home, as well. I would be standing in my living room after a particularly hard day and I would say out loud "This sucks! I am tired of feeling this way," and I would feel better.

There was something about saying it out loud that made it real. I believe it is the difference between rehearsing something in your head versus actually doing it. Occasionally, I will officiate a wedding for friends. I am always honored when they ask me to do it. When I am preparing for the wedding, I am eloquent, charming, funny, and brilliant. As soon as I stand in front of a church full of people and say, "Dearly beloved . . ." I turn into Quasimodo. I'm still brilliant and funny and charming, but Slick is in my head yelling, "GET ME OUTTA HERE!" The same is true when I would ask a woman out on a date. In my head I was suave and irresistible; however, as soon as I would approach a lady, I was interested in and opened my mouth, something like "You have hair . . . I like hair" would come out. I was quite resistible. The point is, saying it in your head and saying it out loud are two very different things.

Meet Your Slick

Once you have decided to live your life, once you have decided that "making it to midnight" is going to happen *every* day, you are halfway home. The second half is giving yourself a reason to live. You need to meet your Slick and make peace with him or her. You need to embrace that part of yourself that you've been fighting against for so long. Before you do that, though, you need to know who is sharing your head with you.

Buckle up! This part is gonna be rough. You have to accept your "Slick" for whom he or she is. Sometimes this realization means that you have to accept some limitations. I know me, and I know Slick. I like to think of myself as a happy-go-lucky, life-of-the-party, talented, professional guy who can do anything I set my mind to. When Slick and I are in sync, I am that guy. Who I *really* am is a man who wants people to like me. I'm a man who crumbles under the silent treatment. I'm a man that will see a look of disappointment in someone I care about and naturally assume I somehow caused it. I'm a man who will hear a friend make a joke about something stupid I did and, while I will laugh at the joke . . . I will spend the next forty-eight hours "beating myself up" for being so stupid. I want acceptance, I want accolades, I want to be told I'm a good boy . . . I want approval.

There is a guy at work who buys a new Porsche every two years. While a Porsche is a beautiful car, it is not a practical car. He and I have similar job titles and responsibilities, so I have an idea of what his salary is. I know I cannot afford a Porsche, and judging by his constant complaining about bills, he cannot either. So why does he have it? He has a Porsche because he wants people to believe he makes more money than he does. He wants to present himself in a way that is not genuine. He is attempting to, with a car he cannot afford, dictate how people perceive him. I realized I was doing the same thing. I was trying to create a perception of being a "tough guy" and that is not who I am.

I remember one time when I was a kid I had a bad wreck on my bicycle. I fractured my collarbone and tore the soft tissue in my shoulder. I was thirteen. I wanted to cry but I did not. I "toughed it out" because I did not want my friends to see me cry. I was creating a perception about myself that was not real. Thirty-four years later, I am unable to sleep on my left side because I did not seek medical attention. Similarly, my attempts to be a tough guy in my day-to-day life caused its share of damage. Nothing caused more damage than trying to put forth a persona that was not me. When I coupled what other people expected from me with the lofty expectations I had of myself, I had created a recipe for failure.

For years, I fought against that part of me. The part of me I now call Slick. Most of my life was spent denying that part of myself that is real. I am a sensitive man. I am not a macho guy; I am not a tough guy or an alpha male. If I bump into someone at the bar, I apologize. If I see a spider in my house, I do my best to catch and release it unharmed. I feel guilty for things I have no control over. If a friend asks me for help, they get it. If I am unable to help, I apologize profusely. When I text or call someone and I don't hear back, I assume I upset them. And you know what? It is okay. It is what makes me . . . me. What is even better is that there are a lot of people who love me for it. Once I accepted that I am not the person that I try to portray and I will never be the person others expect me to be, and started being the person I am, my life got better.

Weathering the Storm

Up to this point, we have talked a lot about how Slick and I co-exist. We have talked about us being equal partners in a lifelong relationship in my head. One thing that separates Slick and me is my knowledge of time. My thinking brain (Jim) is an electrical brain; it is powered by electricity, so as long as there is electricity, there is thinking, and as long as there is thinking, barring any unforeseen circumstance, there will be an awareness of the past, present, and future. My emotional brain (Slick), however, lives purely in the moment. The chemicals that Slick produces will fluctuate throughout the day; this is why we have highs and lows, good and bad moods. These moods are a result of the fluctuation of the chemicals in our limbic system. If we follow this line of reasoning, severe depression and anxiety, while they can last for long periods of time, will have moments of relief. Suicidal thoughts are most prevalent when dips in these chemicals are at their worst. What I found is that these "storms" will pass. If you can weather the storm until midnight, you will live to fight another day.

When I was in the midst of a storm, I needed to count on Jim. During these storms, Slick was flooding our body with chemicals designed to get Jim to do what he wanted. The problem was that when Slick was having what was essentially a panic attack, Jim had to take the wheel. There were times when Slick was in a full-blown tantrum. Up to this point, I have been a proponent of Slick and Jim co-existing equally as roommates, and I stick to that. However, there were times during my years of having roommates that one of them would get really drunk. One roommate, in particular, was an angry drunk. I would get him in the car after a night of drinking and while driving down the highway, he would put his hands over my eyes . . . just to see what would happen. He would kick the car out of gear and one night he even kicked out the windows of his own car. Despite acting like an uncontrollable child, my roommate was still my roommate; however, in his incapacitated state, I had to be the responsible one and get him home in one piece . . . and that's what I did.

Similarly, when your "Slick" has been compromised by a panic attack or severe depression or medication withdrawal, or even drug or alcohol withdrawals, you will experience something similar in your own head. Your emotions will be wildly out of control. *You* will feel out of control, but remember, your "Jim" and your "Slick" are in separate compartments, and since they are in compartments, they can be compartmentalized. This is *not* an easy task, it's difficult, to be honest, but with time and practice, it is possible.

For several months, I was experiencing serious withdrawals from a medication I had been prescribed—a medication that did not work and actually made my symptoms worse. The withdrawal symptoms presented themselves as severe depression with punctuated periods of clarity. These "windows," as I called them, would appear every thirty-six to forty-eight hours and would last for an hour or two. It essentially was like living with a migraine headache all the time with brief one or two hour reprieves. It was during this time that Slick was in top form, before he and I were friends. He would tell me things like "You are going to be like this forever. You should really just end it." Instead of ending it, I decided to track the length of the windows. I noticed over time that the windows were getting longer and longer. Instead of a two-hour window it became a three-hour window. Now, did the length of the windows really matter? Not really, because the times when I was in abject depression were still pretty horrible, however, what it did was give me a reason to live to the next window. "This window was two hours and forty-five minutes. I wonder how long the next one will be?" So instead of spending the next thirty-six to forty-eight hours in misery, I spent that time anticipating the next window.

As I tracked the length of these windows, I also tracked the length between them. Forty-eight hours turned into forty-five hours . . . then forty-one hours and eventually the depression subsided to the point where my depressive episodes may have lasted a few hours and my "windows" became the majority of my life. Now if I am depressed, it is because I have reason to be . . . you know like a normal person.

From what I found, "windows" are a function of benzodiazepine withdrawals. They may also be a function of withdrawing from other chemicals as well. So what do you do if you are dealing with these withdrawals? Find something. Find anything to distract yourself. Now you know that when I say "distract yourself," what I mean is not to silence Slick, because he will be screaming at this point, but instead, give Slick something to focus on, other than the withdrawals. During times like this, I would go for a walk and practiced the mindfulness techniques of noticing every blade of grass, every insect. If you can find a bee or something to watch . . . do it, and do it for as long as you want. When I practiced this technique, I marveled at the majesty of nature, and I talked to Slick about everything we saw. You will feel goofy, but do it. While walking Tahoe, I have said to Slick, "Hey, Slick, check out this bee." There was one time I was having a particularly rough day, so I went to an outdoor restaurant and ordered some pancakes, with the intention of just being outside and trying to clear my head. While I was eating the pancakes, a couple of flies started eating the syrup off the corner of my plate. I put my chin on the table and Slick and I watched them for what felt like hours. I am sure people were staring at me, but at that point, I did not care; Slick and I were in the moment and we were riding it out. Regardless of what the other patrons thought . . . it worked.

There is an old joke that asks, "How do you eat an elephant?" The answer is "one bite at a time." If you struggle with suicidal ideation, forever is a very long time. *Make It to Midnight* is designed to make forever into "one bite at a time." Like Mike said at Dawson Prison so many years ago, "One day is as big a bite of life as I can take."

Know Your Limitations

To quote Dirty Harry, "A man's gotta know his limitations." This is very good advice for people suffering from depression and anxiety as well. I do have some tips and tricks I learned when I was going through these storms. First, realize that your decision-making ability is severely compromised. When these storms hit, you will be in pain, emotional pain, and you will want this pain to stop. One of your first desires may be for some "retail therapy." Do not do it! Do not make any big purchasing decisions while you're in the midst of this; you will regret it. I remember when I was going through a particularly bad storm; I went on Craigslist and bought a car. I thought, "Hey I've been through some hell recently, I deserve a reward." So

I bought a car . . . a freaking car! Those little words "I deserve a reward" can be deadly. When the car arrived at my house, I realized what I had done . . . I had made a bad situation worse. Now I was depressed and I had a car I did not really want or need.

Second, realize you are emotionally raw . . . very raw. You need to share this with people, especially those closest to you. Trust me on this; it is far easier for your loved ones to support you at these times if they know what is going on. It is so much easier to walk in and say, "Hey, honey, my anxiety is at a 'seven' today, and I'm going to try not to let it affect you, but if I am a little punchy, please understand, it is not you. I'm just not feeling myself today." Another thing that I've been told that has really helped my loved ones is this quote, "Sometimes, I need to go off on my own. I'm not sad. I'm not angry. I'm just recharging my batteries." This quote has really helped Sylvia in that it alleviated her feelings that my need to get away was something that she had caused. If you tell those around you what is going on and what to expect, they are much more likely to be accommodating.

Something that is critical is that when you get over the storm, go back to your loved ones and tell them that you are feeling better, and be sure to thank them. This not only lets them know that the storm has passed, but that you are thankful for their support. Imagine if I went to Sylvia every few weeks and told her that I was going through the storm, but then, I never went back and told her when I was feeling better. The only conclusion that she could draw is that I always felt badly.

Recently I read an article in *Psychology Today*, which put forth the hypothesis that depression is contagious. I agree with their assertion. If you tell your loved ones that you are depressed and do not tell them when you feel better, they will not only feel badly for you, but they may feel as if they are failing you because of their inability to help you to feel better. If they only hear that you are depressed and they are unable to help you, they may become depressed themselves. The simple act of telling them that you are having a good day not only tells them that they need not worry about you, but it also gives them the sense of accomplishment that they were, in some part, able to help.

Bring Your Lunch

Earlier, I referenced one of my favorite chapters in the Bible . . . John chapter 6. In John 6, we see Jesus and His disciples sitting on a mountainside looking at a large crowd gathering around them. When Jesus saw the crowd, he asked Philip, "Where shall we buy bread for these people to eat?" Jesus knew what he had planned, but He saw this as an opportunity to teach Philip, the disciples, and us about faith. Philip answered, "It would take more than half a year's wages to buy enough bread for each one to have a bite!" Another disciple, Andrew, then spoke up and said, "Here is a boy with five small barley loaves and two small fish, but how far will they go among so many?" Before we move forward, let's pick this apart. Jesus asked Philip *where* to buy bread, not how, then Andrew answered with where to get bread but now *how* to get enough. This is, in many cases, how we view things, especially with anxiety and depression. We see the problem and we are unable to comprehend a where or a how to solve our problem. In this instance, Jesus is both the where and the how.

What I love most about this story is that Jesus uses a small boy to deliver the food that he uses to feed the multitudes. When Andrew says, "Here is a boy with five small barley loaves and two small fish, but how far will they go among so many?" Jesus then took the bread and fish from the boy, with his permission of course, and gave thanks, and distributed as much as they wanted to those who were seated. He did the same with the fish. When they had enough to eat, he said to his disciples, "Gather the pieces that are left over. Let nothing be wasted." So they gathered them and filled twelve baskets with the pieces of the five barley loaves that were left. Besides Jesus, there are three main players in this scene—Philip, Andrew, and the boy. Jesus asked Philip, "Where shall we buy bread for these people to eat,?" To which Philip replied, "We don't have enough money to buy bread." Philip just told God that they did not have enough money. Have you ever told God that you do not have enough money? I know I have . . . and yet I always seem to have enough for my daily bread. There have been months when all I had money for was bread, but God has always provided. Next we see Andrew who does not have bread, but he sees someone who does. I have been Andrew on numerous occasions, especially in the depths of my depression. I have had moments when I was completely unable to help anyone, but I could point them to someone who could. Andrew did not have bread, but he had faith.

Finally, there is the boy. The boy woke up that morning, just like every other morning. He got some bread and some fish and headed out to hear this Jesus guy speak. He had no idea what the day had in store for him, but when Jesus asked for what he could offer, he gave all he had. This boy saved my life. I used to sit and imagine what it was like for him to just be sitting on the ground and have Jesus walk up and say, "Excuse me, can I have your lunch?" I imagine this little boy looking up innocently, without doubt, without hesitation, without any idea of what Jesus was going to do, and just said, "Here, Jesus, here's my lunch." I want to be that boy; I want his faith. In Matthew 18:2–4 Jesus says,

> He called a little child to him, and placed the child among them. And he said: "Truly I tell you, unless you change and become like little children, you will never enter the kingdom of heaven. Therefore, whoever takes the lowly position of this child is the greatest in the kingdom of heaven.

While I am in no hurry to enter the Kingdom of Heaven, I want my existence on Earth to mirror his. I want Jesus to take whatever I have and use it for His glory. Now, from a personal perspective, try to imagine what the rest of that kid's life was like. He saw Jesus take his lunch and feed thousands with it. Can you imagine the pride that boy felt for the rest of his life? His life was defined by that moment; he is in the Bible! I want to feel that. I want to boast in the Lord as 1 Corinthians 1:26–31 says, because I am that lowly thing that God uses for His glory. How can I be anxious or depressed when God is using me to make the world a better place?

> Brothers and sisters, think of what you were when you were called. Not many of you were wise by human

> *standards; not many were influential; not many were of noble birth. But God chose the foolish things of the world to shame the wise; God chose the weak things of the world to shame the strong. God chose the lowly things of this world and the despised things—and the things that are not—to nullify the things that are, so that no one may boast before him. It is because of him that you are in Christ Jesus, who has become for us wisdom from God—that is, our righteousness, holiness and redemption. Therefore, as it is written: "Let the one who boasts boast in the Lord."*

The point of this story is that we were all put on this earth for a reason. Ending one's life negates God's purpose for us. Sticking around will most likely benefit those who will eventually need you the most. Let your affliction be your testimony. One day you will emerge from the Valley of the Shadow of Death and you will be a light to others. You will be able to serve the next generation. When Jesus was washing the disciple's feet in John 13:7, He said "You do not realize now what I am doing, but later you will understand." For me, that verse rang true for a long time. I was in the depths of my depression and I cried out to God regularly. I asked and begged Him to make it stop, yet I felt my prayers were bouncing off the ceiling. Then I remembered that verse, "You do not realize now what I am doing, but later you will understand." He was right; now I understand.

Hug the Cactus

In 2011, Robert Downey Jr. performed one of the greatest acts of love and compassion for a friend that I have ever seen. Years earlier, he had some problems with addiction and could not get work as an actor. Mel Gibson found out about his situation and gave him a role in a movie that was originally written for Mel. That singular act of faith and kindness restarted his career and allowed him to become the successful star he is today. According to Downey, Gibson did not ask him for repayment or anything for himself; he only asked him to pay the kindness forward and help someone else in the future. Years later, while receiving an acting award, Downey had the opportunity to choose someone to present him with the award. He chose Mel Gibson. It was at this time that Gibson was having his own struggles with addiction and had been shunned by the Hollywood community. While receiving the award, Downey said, "When I couldn't get sober, he told me not to give up hope and encouraged me to find my faith. It didn't have to be his or anyone else's faith, as long as it was rooted in forgiveness. And I couldn't get hired, so he cast me in the lead of a movie that was actually developed for him. He kept a roof over my head, food on the table, and most importantly, he said if I accepted responsibility for my wrongdoing and embraced that part of my soul that was ugly—hugging the cactus he called it—he said that if I hugged the cactus long enough, I'd become a man of some humility and my life would take on a new meaning. And I did...and it worked."

Downey continued, "I did, and it worked. All he asked in return was that someday I help the next guy in some small way. It is reasonable to assume that at the time he didn't imagine the next guy would be him, or that someday was tonight. So anyway, on this special occasion, and in light of the recent holidays, including Columbus Day, I would ask that you join me, unless you are completely without sin in which case you picked the wrong f——ing industry, in forgiving my friend his trespasses and offering him the same clean slate you have offered me, allowing him to continue his great and ongoing contribution to our collective art without shame. He's hugged the cactus long enough."

When I heard that, it resonated with me. I had been fighting Slick most of my life. I had been fighting against that part of me that I thought was my enemy. It turns out he and I had the same goal, we just wanted to be happy and at peace. It is amazing to realize that the lack of peace I felt was my choice . . . to fight against myself! As soon as I hugged Slick . . . my cactus, my life improved in ways I could not imagine.

You, or someone you know, might be dealing with something inside of you that you desperately want to change. It could be depression, or anxiety, or an addiction. Whatever it is, your spirit and flesh are at cross-purposes. In Mark 3:25, Jesus said, "If a house is divided against itself, that house cannot stand." In my journey, I had to—*had to*—accept myself for whom I was and where I was. I had, at a minimum, depression and anxiety; the rest was up for debate. Slick and I were battle-weary from years of fighting against each other. It took me years to acquire those two diagnoses, although I could see evidence of them in my childhood as well. It took years to get here and it was going to take time to get back to where I wanted to be. The first thing I had to do was admit and accept where I was. If I told you to take a journey of five hundred miles you would need to know two things: where you are starting and where you are ending. When you sign up for a class, or a college degree, or a trip, you get two pieces of information, the beginning and the end. If you and the college do not agree on a start date, you won't be starting. If you and your travel agent do not agree on an airport and a time for your vacation to start, you're not taking a vacation. Imagine if you got a job and the new boss did not tell you when you start or where to report, it would be a very short tenure. Without at least an acknowledgement of where you are mentally, you cannot effectively move forward.

Slick and I had to make amends. We had to learn how to live together, which meant that I had to "hug my cactus" and realize that there were parts of me that needed to change . . . and I am changing them. When I was in therapy, my counselors advised me that I needed to dictate to Slick what I wanted him to change, and force it to happen. As you can imagine, that led to further division in my head. It wasn't until I made him my partner in this journey that I was able to find happiness. I had to acknowledge that Slick had rights and I had to respect him, or we would both be miserable. In my life, I found that I wanted to do everything, and be everything to everyone, wanting to make everyone happy. There were times when I had to decline playing guitar at church because the stress of learning five new songs in a week was more than he was prepared to take on. I had to look at His situation and sometimes make difficult decisions of what was best for Us. I am a six-foot-tall man; I have a dog that is less than a foot tall. His legs are, at best, four inches long. If I want to go for a five-mile run, I cannot take Tahoe with me; he physically cannot make that run. I can attempt to drag him along, but that would be abusive. The same thing was true for Slick. He was exhausted and burned out from constantly working and going to school to try to get ahead. He just could not keep up.

Whether I was born with the chemical imbalance that led to my current situation, or it was thrust upon me, or if it was just my own poor decisions is irrelevant. I realized that what mattered was that I was there, sitting on my bed with a gun in my hand and had a decision to make. I thank God every day for my decision to "make it to midnight." It is a never-ending journey, but it does get easier. Trust me on this, there comes a point where you look back at where you were and where you are now, and the road ahead doesn't look so bad. There will come a day when you start seeing the beauty in the world around you. You will start to hear the birds again and even marvel at a bee hovering over a flower. In some ways, your "cactus" can be a gift, because once you have hugged the thorns off your cactus, your life will be better than it has ever been. When your "cactus" starts hugging you back, and your spirit lives in harmony with your flesh, you will enjoy the world around you like never before. There is nothing that feels like going from rock bottom to the top of the world. I'm not saying that you have to hit rock bottom to enjoy life, but when you finally climb out of the valley you are in, even normal days are a joy.

Evaluate Your Life

There may be a gap or a canyon between who you want to be and who you truly are. I know in my work with addicts, once they admit the problem, they want the problem fixed *now*, but unfortunately, our brains do not work that way. The hard truth of addiction, depression, or anxiety is that it took years to create the situation, and it may take years to correct. One thing I had to come to terms with is that whoever was responsible for my situation, be it my parents or me, or an ex, or a random stranger, was irrelevant. Read this and read it again . . . if you blame someone else for your situation, you give away your ability to fix it. Now read it again. If you blame someone else for your situation, YOU GIVE AWAY YOUR ABILITY TO FIX IT! An analogy for "fixing" this is the following: if my car gets nailed by an uninsured motorist, I am stuck with the tab. Does it suck? Absolutely. Is it fair? Nope. So I have two choices, either I just live without a car and complain about it, or I do what it takes to get my car back on the road. I do it. If someone in your past did you wrong and caused you pain, I'm sorry, I really am, but only *you* can fix it.

For me, the first step was to accept that Slick was totally burned out. My dog Tahoe is my best friend in the world; he's very intelligent and very loyal. However, Tahoe has separation anxiety, and he expresses it by chewing up the blinds and door frames in the house when I leave him alone. One day, Tahoe had chewed up a door in the house because he was mad at me for leaving . . . which used to happen fairly regularly. Something happened with Tahoe prior to my adopting him that makes him afraid to be alone. I have to accept that about Tahoe and *then* we can start working on it. If I yell at him every time he chews up the door, he will actually become more anxious and do it more, or worse, he will begin to fear me rather than love me. It would be pointless to find the people who caused his separation anxiety, because he's now my dog, and I have to accept him as the dog he is now. Tracking them down would do absolutely no good; in fact, if I showed up and started berating them for causing my dog's separation anxiety, they would probably call the cops. So instead of blaming his previous owners, if there were any, I have chosen to accept and love him for whom he is now. What I have had to do is to accept this is part of him and work with him in love to show him that his home is safe. We live there together, and I will always come home. After coming home every day consistently for nine years now, his door-chewing has almost been completely eliminated.

The same holds true for Slick. Slick is emotional, not logical. Slick and I talk to each other, but it is not in a reasoning way; it is in a nurturing and reassuring way. When I found out the company

I worked for had been sold, Slick freaked! Now I could have said to Slick, "We have had a job since we were fifteen and we will find one." That is not reassuring; that is logical. I am quoting facts rather than understanding his feelings. Rather than pull out my resume and show Slick how we had never been without a job despite this being the ninth company to close out from under us, I acknowledged and validated his feelings. I said, "Slick, this sucks (validation)." Then I said, "We will get through this, we always have. I know it is harder now that we are single and older, but we planned for this. We saved for this, we are ready for this (reassurance)."

Why do I talk to slick this way? Jim, my logical brain, already knows this information, but Slick does not deal in information, he deals in emotion. He is afraid for our future, and if I (Jim) were to invalidate his feelings and then essentially yell at him for feeling that way, I am harming myself. Have you ever heard of the phrase "beating yourself up"? Well, that is exactly what you are doing, and by doing so, you're making a bad situation worse. When my Slick heard that the company we worked for was closing, he panicked. Fortunately, I had been practicing the principles in this book, so while we got nervous for a little while, we quickly resolved it. This company closing situation is happening right now. I will be without a job in less than a month, and despite having all the diagnoses I have, I'm good with it. I am concerned about it, but to an appropriate degree. That, ladies and gentlemen, is what freedom feels like. No matter what happens, Slick and I will be fine.

One of my diagnoses is attention deficit disorder. I struggle with it constantly. What ADD, by definition, means is that your attention is elsewhere. Well, honestly, that can be caused by just about anything. For example, if you are having an anxiety attack at the store and you leave your wallet on the counter, try your best not to "beat yourself up" over it. What happened was that your Slick was in some sort of distress when you were at the store. You were expending your energy to either try to calm him down, or more likely you were expending most of your energy putting on a front so no one around you knew you were having an anxiety attack. Either way, your logical brain was focusing on something other than where your wallet was.

The worst thing you can do at this point is to get angry at yourself and tell yourself you're stupid or incompetent. Your emotional brain is already in distress; why would you want to add to that? Just tell your Slick, "Hey, these things happen, we will go back and get it. Hopefully someone took it to the lost and found." The point is, do not wish for what isn't; accept what is.

One example of this is when I talk with someone with depression and they *all* say the exact same thing: "I don't know why I'm depressed; so many people are so much worse off than I am, and yet they are happy." That is the absolute worst thing you can say to yourself. Why? Well, let's break that sentence down to its essence. What you are really telling yourself is that you are weak and that you are not strong enough to handle what life has thrown at you. This is not true. As anyone with depression or anxiety knows . . . we are definitely *not* weak. Depression has nothing to do with how successful you are emotionally, financially, or relationally. If that was the case, there would be no rich, successful, or married people struggling with depression. Instead of telling yourself that you should feel better because you are better off than others, why not express gratitude to God for what he has given you, then accept who you are and where you are right now.

I volunteered with a dog rescue for several years in South Texas. My job at this rescue was to take dogs who had been adopted in one city to their new home in a different city. I got a call one weekend to pick up a basset hound in Waco and transport him to Austin. I got to Waco and picked him up. His name was Red; he was a big red basset hound who was as sweet as could be with a great disposition. The lady at the shelter handed me a single piece of paper with Red's history and everything anyone knew about this sweet dog was on that one piece of paper. There was not a lot—just his breed, estimated age, and a few shot records. According to his history, the reason for his being at the shelter was "owner surrender/possible neglect." This broke my heart. Who could do this to such a sweet dog? I pulled out of the parking lot with Red. Before I got to the highway, I heard him snoring in the back seat. I was amazed! How could this dog who had no idea who I was, and no idea where he was going, be so relaxed as to fall asleep in my car in under a minute? I was actually envious of Red at this point. What I came to realize on the drive is that Red was happy and relaxed because where he was now was better than where he had been. Next time you compare yourself to someone who is homeless or in what you consider a bad situation and decide you are envious because they appear happier than you are, remember, it could be as simple as where they are now is better than where they were.

When you tell yourself you should feel better because other people are living in a less desirable situation than you, you are, in essence, scolding your Slick. You are telling that child inside of you that he or she is broken. Something that is really interesting about mental illness is that we assume all people are created equal. We do that in no other arena of the human condition. We gauge each other by our diversity. We compare ourselves to each other and categorize ourselves based on height, weight, eye color, ethnicity, and socioeconomic standards. We compare our neocortices with IQ tests, but we do not do this with our emotions. If human IQs can vary so widely from intellectually disabled to genius, why do we not classify emotions in the same way? We try to with certain assessments in the mental health field, but those assessments are generally given *after* you walk into the clinic. What about the people who never visit the clinic?

Einstein is credited with saying, "Everyone is a genius. But if you judge a fish by its ability to climb a tree, it will live its whole life believing that it is stupid." I believe the same is true for our emotions. We are *not* all created equally. I had the opportunity to work as a trainer at NASA's Jet Propulsion Laboratory (JPL). I am a very smart guy; I was a member of Mensa. I went to JPL and immediately realized I was not the smartest one in the room. I am not a rocket scientist, and there's a good chance you are not either. I can say that I do not have the intellectual ability to be a rocket scientist. I am smart? Yes, but they are smarter. That was an assessment I made about myself. This realization did not make me feel deficient; it just is. People are very willing to accept their physical and intellectual differences. Those of us who are less than six feet, five inches tall are usually willing to accept that we will not play in the NBA. However, we do not call that a "height disorder." Those of us who do not score in the top percentiles of standardized tests accept the fact that medical school is probably not in our future; however, we do not refer to ourselves as "intellectually deficient." Just because we do not possess the emotional capacity to do something does *not* mean we have a disorder any more than it means you are mentally deficient because you are not a rocket scientist. It is how you are made; God made you the way you are for a reason.

Try to imagine the world that God created us in. He created us in a hostile world. The Bible is replete with God's people going to battle. However, declaring war in biblical times was not the same as it is now. In biblical times, the invading army would set up camp in the country they wanted to invade. They would send in an emissary to negotiate terms of coexistence or surrender. If negotiations failed, then a war would ensue. The invading army and the defending army needed three types of people to be successful. They needed a leader, someone who represented the army. This person needed to be a gifted negotiator. Secondly, the army needed soldiers. These soldiers needed to be warriors. They needed to be aggressive, driven by competition, and skilled in battle. Finally, the army needed support. This support came in the form of compassionate people who were skilled in healing. I am not a leader, even though I am a very intelligent man. I am not a warrior, even though I am physically strong. I am compassionate. I am built to help people heal. However, before I could heal others I had to follow Luke's advice in Luke 4:23: "Physician, heal thyself."

One of my "attributes" is that I am not comfortable with uncertainty. I am not the guy who can just quit his job and run off to Thailand just because I want an adventure. I envy that guy, but I am not that guy. Slick needs stability. Slick needs a steady income stream. Many people see that as a weakness and something I need to change. People will tell me, "You need to become more comfortable with uncertainty." This reminds me of an episode of the Tyra Banks show (don't judge me). In this episode, Tyra was facing her phobia of dolphins. She forced herself to get in a pool with dolphins and was in abject panic the entire time. Was she facing her fear or just torturing her limbic system? I kept thinking, "Hey, Tyra, dolphins are fairly easy to avoid . . . how about just not going where the dolphins are." I accepted that Slick does not like uncertainty, so I do my best to avoid it, pretty simple. I used to try to "face my fears." I then realized my fears are designed to help me. They are placed in my life to teach me what God designed me for. Some people see their fears as hurdles to overcome; I see them as guardrails to keep me on the path God has laid out for me.

Social media is overflowing with people, mostly celebrities, who are preaching the gospel of facing your fears, jumping off, quitting your dull life and chasing your dreams. I am all for doing those things. The implication is that you are a failure if you do not leave your comfortable life and chase your dreams. Jim Carrey delivered an amazing college graduation speech where he recounted his father being laid off as an accountant. He said, "You can fail at what you hate, or you can fail at what you love." Again, I would love to be the guy who quits his comfy IT job and runs off to follow my dreams. However, emotionally, I am not built to do that. I believe most people who suffer from mental illness are also not equipped to make that leap. If they (we) were, there would be a lot more comedians. I am not discouraging you or myself for not following my dreams; I am encouraging you to not think less of yourself if you choose a safe career. Asking me to jump to a new career during the depths of my depression would be like asking the survivors of the *Titanic* to swim the English Channel. It is not that we are weak; we have just been strong for too long. One of Freud's less famous quotes is "If you can't do it, give up!"

The flipside to this scenario is when people with depression or anxiety pursue their dreams in an effort to counteract their affliction. As I am writing this part of the book, I am on vacation in Thailand. I may not be the guy who quits his job and moves to Thailand, but I will definitely vacation here. Last night, I was walking around the streets of Bangkok, and I saw a legless man lying facedown on the sidewalk. He had a small bowl on the ground in front of him for passersby to drop change into. As I walked by (and dropped twenty baht into his bowl), I could not help but think about the daily struggle of this man. What I am going to write next may sound cold and calloused, but that is not my intention. I am merely dissecting suicidal ideation from a completely objective point of view. If I look at this man on the sidewalk, logically I could make the argument that he is a candidate for suicide. He has no legs, no job, and from all indications, no chance to change either of those circumstances . . . and yet he makes his way to his spot on the sidewalk every day surviving on the generosity of others.

Contrast that with an article I read recently, "A 47-year-old financial company executive was killed Wednesday when he jumped from a luxury apartment building on the Upper West Side, authorities said." We have a man who is most likely a multimillionaire living in the very definition of luxury who chooses to end his life and a man with no job, no home and no hope who fights and literally crawls on the sidewalk each day to survive. Society would be tempted to call one man weak for ending his life while calling the other man brave for struggling to survive. They would most likely applaud the man on the street in Bangkok for his tenacity and perseverance in the face of such adversity. If his story reached the west, I have no doubt that several fundraising campaigns would spring to life to assist this man, to which I would happily donate. Contrast that with the executive who chose to end his life. I am sure the response to that would not be as understanding. I would expect the responses to be laden with confusion as to how a man who had reached the pinnacle of financial and vocational success could have chosen to take his own life. When people talk about a person who has ended their own life they often say "He took the easy way out" or "He just passed his problems onto someone else" or "How could he do this to his family?"

Allow me to rewrite the story briefly. Today I saw a legless man on a Bangkok street begging for change. I marveled at his tenacity and perseverance in the face of such adversity. When I returned to my hotel, I read an article that began "A 47-year-old financial company executive was pronounced dead on Wednesday when had a massive heart attack in his luxury apartment on the Upper West Side, authorities said." See the difference? I even see the bias in the wording of the article. The use of the words "luxury apartment" biases the reader to view the man as privileged, further perpetuating the notion that people who choose suicide are weak. When a person dies from an identifiable disease such as cancer or heart disease, regardless of socioeconomic status, they are mourned. When a person of privilege or success dies of suicide, they are viewed with derision. What is even more disturbing is later in the article we read, "Oh my God, another one?" he said in disbelief. "Somebody committed suicide a few months ago . . . on the other side of the building. I can't believe it. It's almost exactly the same thing, but just around the side." So two people who live in exclusive New York apartments decide to commit suicide within months of one another and crippled beggars in Bangkok struggle to survive day after day, year after year. Quite a juxtaposition.

Let me offer an alternate hypothesis. I believe, based on personal experience, that the successful person who commits suicide (as I am a successful person who almost did) is born with a predisposition for depression. That person who is born with this predisposition spends their entire life looking for ways to combat their sadness. One way they choose to combat their depression is to attempt to achieve financial and vocational success. They (we) believe that by achieving this success we will feel accomplished and no longer depressed. This makes complete sense as our limbic system is designed to reward success with the feel good chemical dopamine. The successful hunter in ancient times received dopamine after a successful hunt as an encouragement to achieve that success again just as the successful salesman will receive dopamine after closing a big sale. What happened to me, and what I believe happened to the two people who ended their lives in New York, was that they always had depression and suicidal thoughts. They attempted to assuage those proclivities through financial success. They lived their lives with the completely logical belief that when they achieved their goal their depression would subside. When they reached their goal and the depression was still present they came to the conclusion they would never be free from depression . . . so they chose to free themselves.

Instead of the article reading, "A 47-year-old financial company executive was killed Wednesday when he jumped from a luxury apartment building on the Upper West Side, authorities said." We could rewrite the article and the paradigm to read more like, "A 47-year-old financial company executive lost his battle with depression on

Wednesday when he jumped from a luxury apartment building on the Upper West Side, authorities said."

Another assessment I had to make about myself is that I do not have the emotional capacity to be a manager or executive. I'm not going to say I have an "anxiety disorder," I just do not possess the ability to withstand the stress that is thrust upon someone who is in charge of a business. I know that Slick would be in a constant state of panic every day. He would constantly worry about the business, the employees, whether I was a good manager or not? That is the way he is built. I have the intellectual capacity to be a CEO, but not the emotional capacity. I am not an emotionally weak person, but I am an emotionally sensitive person. I am far more suited to be an employee rather than a leader; that is where my emotional strength lies.

After I received my bachelor's degree in economics in 1995, I became a stock broker. This meant I was in sales, and by extension, I would be living on commission. My father was in sales most of my life, so I was no stranger to the ups and downs of commission sales. My father was an excellent salesman and did very well, so there was no reason for me to think I would not excel in this field. Slick disagreed. As soon as I started selling, Slick began voicing his doubts. Finally, Slick won the battle and I pursued a career in computers. Let me be clear: I did not fail as a salesperson. I actually did very well, but the stress of not having a steady income was more than I was willing to accept. I was not emotionally built to be in sales. I could have fought against Slick and forced myself to continue, and while I may have been financially successful, I would have been emotionally miserable.

Many of us are in careers we are not emotionally built for. Just because you are good at math does not mean you enjoy it. Just because you are the top salesman does not mean that you are happy. If there is one word I wish I could remove from the English language, it is the word "should."

"Oh, you're good at math, you *should* be an accountant."

"Oh, you like kids, you *should* be a teacher." I am not going to tell you what I believe you should or should not do, but I will tell you this, when I asked Slick what he wanted to do and actually listened, I became a lot happier. Several of my friends have asked me over the years, "Hey, why aren't you in management by now?" They ask me like it is expected. Like there is an unwritten career path for all people in my industry. Slick showed me his boundaries, and I respected them. He is not able to accept the stress that comes with sales and living on commission. He is not able to disassociate enough to be in a management position. Slick is not someone who can say, "It's not personal, it's just business." Some people are able to do that, but I cannot.

Sylvia is an intellectual woman. She holds a PhD in education. She is a wonderful writer, and she is extremely knowledgeable about literacy and how best to help children acquire their knowledge of it. Sylvia previously worked as a reading specialist for an elementary school and, after graduating with her PhD, it seemed logical that her next step "should" be to pursue a career in higher education. As luck would have it, she was able to secure a position as a professor at a local university. It was during this year that she found out some things about herself: first, she enjoyed the teaching aspect of this career. She thrived on her ability to help her students learn the practical application of the theory on which she lectured. Second, she completely disliked the university's expectation to publish research and basically, "Write on demand."

After months of reflection, Sylvia has decided to return to her former career of reading specialist. This has confirmed her understanding that working with children and their teachers is where her heart and abilities belong for now. This was not an easy decision for her to make. As she has said to me in many of our discussions, "You get a PhD to teach at the college level and to make your word known to a larger audience, contributing to the educational community in ways that you are not able to at the public school level. I should want to do this. Something must be wrong with me that I don't see myself in higher education." Is Sylvia intelligent enough to continue on the road of university professor? Absolutely. Does she want to? Probably not right now. At this time, she is in the process of coming to terms with the fact that she is not emotionally built for this type of career.

Military snipers have a saying, "You can run, but you will only die tired." The same holds true for our emotional selves. I can run from the reality that Slick has limitations, but I will only die tired.

Those of us who are more emotionally sensitive (I am going to stop saying anxiety disorder or depression) are blessed with the ability to know what is a good fit for us and what is not. What we have to do is listen to what our Slick says and then make a decision based on all the information. If I am good at math, but Slick hates math, we will not be happy. If I am a very social IT person, many would say I "should" go into management. I tried it, and Slick hated it. The stress was too much for him. Rather than force Slick to go into management, I accepted his input, and I am not in management. Just because someone is financially or vocationally successful, does not mean they are emotionally successful. I will take emotional success over financial and vocational success any day.

If You're Going through Hell . . . KEEP GOING!

Our limbic system is wired to avoid pain and seek pleasure. It is built to encourage us to continue behaviors that keep us alive and further the species. This is why dogs will learn tricks for treats; a dog learns that if he sits when his person says "sit," he will get a treat . . . so he sits. What do you suppose would happen if the dog was punished for sitting then punished for standing, then punished for lying down? The dog would be confused and probably anxious and depressed. Following that logic, what do you think our limbic system, which is remarkably similar to a dog's brain does when we are going through rough times? When we go through hell, no matter what we do, it seems to be the wrong thing. Misery is waiting around every corner. If we go to work, we are depressed, if we stay home, we are depressed, if we go to a concert, we are depressed . . . nothing we do seems to make it stop, so we do what a dog would do—nothing. You may have a desire to sleep all day because life is painful. You may have the desire to withdraw from society and stay at home as much as possible because nothing but pain awaits you. Please fight that temptation because the only thing worse than going *through* hell is staying there.

The problem with going *through* tough times is that we never know how long the tough times will last. We never know how long the *"through"* is going to be. However, if we adopt a "make it to midnight" attitude and just do that . . . just make it to midnight every day . . . you can declare victory every day at 12:01 AM! Every day is a victory because you made it!

I know you may be thinking, "Jim, it's harder than that." Yeah, it is, making it through twenty-four hours in constant pain is not for the weak, but it is possible. The reason I stuck so steadfastly to the "make it to midnight" mantra is because I could inventory what I needed for that day and put my anxiety at a little bit of ease. Remember what I said before; anxiety had robbed me of my future and depression had stolen my past. Let's focus a moment on anxiety. For me, it's fear of the future, fear that I will not be able to pay my bills, fear that I will not be able to take care of myself in the future. This is, by no means, an irrational fear; we all get older and we will all need money and other people to survive. But if you have food and water for today, then try to focus on that. "Make it to midnight" is a total mind-set, it's a mind-set based on your ability to just make it to midnight. I have a tattoo on my right shoulder that has this verse in it, Matthew 6:34, which says, "Therefore do not worry about tomorrow, for tomorrow will worry about itself. Each day has enough trouble of its own." I live that every day.

Our Daily Bread

One of the great things about Jesus is His clarity. In Matthew 6 Jesus tells us how to pray . . . He tells us *exactly* how to pray.

"This, then, is how you should pray:
'Our Father in heaven, hallowed be your name,
your Kingdom come, your will be done, on earth
as it is in heaven. Give us today our daily bread.
And forgive us our debts, as we also have forgiven

*our debtors. And lead us not into temptation, but
deliver us from the evil one.'"*

Back in 1994, I was homeless for a while. I had made a series of bad decisions, and I ended up living in an empty building in Austin, Texas, with a bunch of other people. While I was not proud of the title "homeless," I chose the moniker "residentially challenged." I always thought that being homeless was the worst thing that could happen to a person, and for many people it is, but for me, it was one of the greatest experiences of my life. I was free, and above all, I was happy. I was also in my early twenties and had no children to support so that helped a lot. What surprised me the most is that I was living with people, many of whom chose to be homeless! You may be asking, "Why would anyone choose to be homeless?" They did not want to follow anyone else's rules. They lived life one day at a time.

There was a guy named Black who lived in the building with me. I never knew his real name, but he chose to be called Black. I asked him why he chose that name and he said that depressed people feel a darkness inside and he never wanted to feel that way, so he decided to name himself Black as a reminder of how he never wanted to feel. He called me Squirrel, for some reason; I thought it was better not to know why. Black was the essence of freedom; Black had life figured out. He was a very street smart and intelligent man in his early twenties. He was not, from what I could tell, suffering from any mental illness, other than constantly stealing my socks. Black had his life figured out; he had figured that he needed $40 a day to live—he needed $20 for food and $20 for pot. Please do not misunderstand; I am not condoning the use of marijuana at all, what I am saying is that Black enjoyed food and pot and that is as far as his concern went. He did not worry about bills or a job because he had neither. He was never concerned about tomorrow, if he made his $40 by noon his day was done and he enjoyed the rest of the day. He truly lived by the mantra "give me this day my daily bread." Again I'm talking about the food, not the pot.

Black was a philosophical guy, to say the least, but his wisdom was unquestionable. There were many people there like Black and I had the incredible opportunity to learn from them. Unfortunately, I had forgotten many of those lessons in life, but with the help of this book, I am relearning them. I thought I had hit rock bottom when in reality I had been given a private audience with some of the most brilliant minds I have ever known, I was just too naïve to realize it. One night we were talking about life and happiness, and I was still astounded that these men and women who lived in this building had chosen this life. I told them that I wanted to finish my degree and get a job and have a good and successful life, and after assuring them that I meant no insult, I told them that living in an empty building was not my goal; it was just a result of some poor decisions and I wanted to get on with my life. One of the older gentlemen there asked me, "Jim, what is your idea of a successful life?" I told him that I wanted my degree, a good job, a nice house, and a wife someday . . . and a dog. Definitely a dog. He then asked me a very profound question. He asked, "If you were incarcerated and thrown in prison what would that look like?" I told him it would be miserable. I would be put in a cell and I would have people in uniforms controlling every aspect of my life. I would be told when I could eat, when I could shower, when I could go outside, if at all, I would have no control of my life, and above all, I would lose all the years that I spent in prison. He then said, "So how is that different from a job in a cubicle?" I'm still working on the answer to that one.

We are told from an early age that getting a good job, putting in our thirty to forty years, climbing the corporate ladder, getting a house, a dog, and two to three kids is the ticket to happiness. For many people that is true, but it may not be true for you. What if what you are told will bring you happiness actually makes you miserable? Jim Carrey said something profound in a college graduation speech, he said, "You can fail at what you hate, or you can fail at what you love . . . why not do what you love?" Maybe you are a person who is happy going to your job every day, and if you are, keep doing it. What I am saying is not to be afraid to look at alternatives.

The Importance of Friends

Some people say, "God will not give you more than you can handle." I believe that is an untrue statement. I believe while God will not give you more than you can handle, life will. Life will give you more than you can handle alone. God will give you people to help you carry your burden. Ecclesiastes 4:9–10 states,

> *Two are better than one, because they have a good return for their labor: If either of them falls down, one can help the other up. But pity anyone who falls and has no one to help them up.*

I use the example of Robert Downey Jr. and Mel Gibson for an important reason. Robert Downey Jr. needed help badly and Mel Gibson was there for him. It was just a few short years later that Mel Gibson needed help and Robert Downey Jr. was there for him. It is cyclical. When I was in the depth of my depression, I had people who were there for me, people who were professionals, and people who were friends. Now just a few short years later, I am the counselor, professionally, for my friends. I believe in the power of counseling to help people, but at its essence, counseling is a meeting of one neocortex and another neocortex. When I counsel people or when I am the client, I am speaking to the neocortex of my client or the counselor's neocortex is speaking to me. While this is beneficial, the part of the brain that holds the limbic system is not in the conversation. If Slick is the one who is hurting, it makes sense to address that part of the brain. As a counselor, it is frowned upon to have physical contact with a client. Having my client put their head in my lap while we talk is not ethical, we are supposed to maintain a professional detachment, but sometimes a five-second hug does more than a fifty-minute counseling session.

It is crucial that you have friends you can count on, but what is also crucial is how you treat them and how they treat you. Sometimes you have to teach people how to treat you. The first step for me moving toward recovery was "hugging the cactus." Hugging your cactus in your own head is hard, but the next step is introducing that cactus to someone. Every day, millions of people suffer in silence from depression or anxiety. It is either out of embarrassment, shame, pride, or maybe a sense that no one will care. Perhaps they do not want to be a burden or simply because they do not know how to effectively communicate how they feel. Perhaps it is because they are afraid that no one will believe them or that their feelings will be invalidated. This is the next cactus to embrace.

Choose someone you can confide in about your situation. This is going to be difficult because it requires a large amount of vulnerability and vulnerability can get you hurt. However, having someone you can be accountable to is an invaluable asset. I had a couple of friends who knew my situation and they knew how close to the edge I was. They were amazing and helped me through some very difficult times. I learned some very valuable lessons from them on how to treat a friend in that situation and how to teach them how to treat me.

The first thing that almost always happens when one person tells a friend about their problems, whether its depression or anxiety, or which shoes to buy, is that the friend will reply with something like "Well, what you need to do is . . ." or "What I would do is . . ." or my personal favorite, "What do you have to be depressed about?" When one person confides in another about a problem with depression or anxiety, they are not looking for a solution; they are looking for validation. The hardest thing to learn about depression and anxiety is that they may not have an identifiable cause, and they probably do not. That's why they call it mental illness because you feel badly for no reason! What I had to do with my friends is to make a deal with them. I told that them when I talk to them about my situation, they were to ask one question and one question only, and that was "Do you need me to listen, or do you need me to fix it?" The answer was always "I need you to listen."

I knew full well my depression and anxiety made no sense, and I had no reason to be depressed, but it did not change the fact that I was. I needed someone to give me permission to be depressed. I needed my friends to tell me it was okay to feel the way I felt, that

I had the right to. It is counterintuitive, but if you allow yourself to be depressed or anxious and you allow yourself to feel it, it passes. Many people feel depressed or anxious then get angry at themselves for feeling that way, they will tell me they feel weak. Then they try to suppress that feeling, and in doing so, they make the feeling worse. Think about it. You start off with a depressed person who gets angry for being depressed. Now you have an angry, depressed person who is frustrated because they cannot get over the depression! Just telling another human being, "I am really depressed today" and hearing them say, "I'm sorry you are feeling that way" can do wonders; try it.

One thing about friends is that you can burn them out. Let's face it; no one likes to hang out with someone who is down all the time. You need to treat your relationships with your friends almost like a bank account. With a bank account, you can only pull money out if you have money in the account. You are going to have bad days, even bad weeks, but there will be some positive times, even if it's just fifteen minutes, make sure to tell your friend. I learned this lesson the hard way. It had been a few months and I was in my own pool of pity, and every time I talked with one particular friend, I was always telling her how down I was. This is normal; this is human nature. If I felt bad, I would call her and then I would feel better. So logically, Slick realized that calling her made him feel better, so he would always call her when he felt bad. Seems simple enough. Then one day, she said, "You never ask me how I'm doing." I kinda felt like a jerk. However, I was far enough in my journey of reconciling with Slick that I didn't beat him up for it, he and I had a talk. From then on, every time I called her I asked, "Hey, how's your day?"

So after a short talk, Slick and I decided that we would call her when we felt bad, but we would also call when we felt good. We would call just to say "hi," we would call if she posted something cool on Facebook, we would call or text to say we were having a good day. We started acting like normal friends, and over time, the depressed calls decreased and the "normal" calls increased. Now, a couple of years later, we just talk. I didn't fake it till I made it. I had a specific goal, my goal was to have a normal friendship with the person who was my emotional pillar. I achieved that goal.

Something else I identified in my life were the people who were taking too much energy from me. It was very hard for me to admit that I had people in my life that were my friends but were mainly my friends because they could come to me with problems and I would make them feel better. One very important lesson I learned is that you have to teach people how to treat you. When I was the one seeking help, my friend did that to/for me, she said, "How come you never ask me how I am doing?" That was a fair question from her, and it is a fair question to ask anyone who is your friend as well. I am an IT professional by trade and a part-time counselor. As an IT professional, I have many friends and family who will ask me for technology help. I do not mind doing it for them, but I cannot accommodate all the requests and still have a life. If I fixed every computer, phone, DVD player, or car stereo that I was asked to, I would never sleep or eat; I have to say no. The same is true for emotional support, if you have people in your life who constantly use you for emotional support, consider it a compliment, but also consider telling them you need a break as well.

People whom I called "emotional vampires" were easy to identify; whenever they called, I would sigh and decide whether to answer the phone or not. Some got to the point where I would just not answer and there were a couple I had to block. Many people with anxiety and depression have it because they do too much for others and not enough for themselves. I had to give myself permission to say no. It was difficult, as I was used to doing for others, but it was an important part of my healing. You do not have to eliminate these friends from your life; you may just need a break, some "me" time.

Don't Fake It

People will tell you, "Fake it till you make it!" They will tell you that if you just think happy thoughts you will be happy. While we can improve our state of mind through changing our thought patterns, this is not an instantaneous change, it takes time. If you see happiness as a goal, instead of pretending to be happy, it becomes far more achievable. I believe that we should identify that goal. Once the goal has been identified, we should develop a strategy to work toward a goal. If you "fake it till you make it," you know you're faking it! When you want to improve your quality of life either by dealing with your anxiety and depression or by kicking an addiction, you have a clearly defined goal to work toward. You have a vision in your head when you look in the mirror and like the person looking back at you. It is an amazing feeling! When someone decides to go to college, or learn a trade or acquire a skill, they are deciding to make a change to improve themselves. They have knowledge of where they are and they have a vision of where they want to be in the future. For example, if someone decides they want to be a lawyer, they know they need to get a college degree first, so they plan for that eventuality and start along that path. Then, they go to law school and finally pass the bar exam. Then voila, they are a lawyer. In starting their journey, they are not pretending to be a lawyer; they are working toward that goal. From the day you start college until you graduate, you are learning. You're not faking that you're going to be a doctor or lawyer or accountant; you're training for it. The same is true on a road to recovery, there is no faking it; you have a vision of where you want to be and you are working toward that goal.

Working toward a life where you are at peace with your limbic system is a long road, and there will be times when you have setbacks; that is natural and normal. Every day is precious and none can be replaced . . . but some will suck. When I got off Ambien, I hit a new low. I hit depths of depression I did not think were possible; every fiber of my being wanted nothing but for all of it to end. I did anything I could think of to mitigate the pain, but in the end, I just had to get through it and "make it to midnight." It was at this time that I bought a digital watch and set it to military time so I could actually see how much time I had in each day, how far away midnight was. I discovered something during this time; I discovered internet forums. I found a great site called benzobuddies.com. I don't know if it is still in existence, but it helped me on many really tough days. After getting off Ambien, I would be horribly depressed for twenty-four to forty-eight hours, but for one or two hours a day, I would have moments of normalcy. These moments would be like the eye of a hurricane, it would be horrible depression punctuated with an hour or two of my brain being functional, then without warning it would hit again. This went on for several months, and it was unrelenting. Because of benzobuddies.com, I found other people who were experiencing this phenomenon as well; they called them "windows." These were windows of clarity that people who were having benzodiazepine withdrawals experienced. My doctor, having never heard of benzodiazepine withdrawal, diagnosed me with bipolar disorder.

Having diagnosed me with bipolar 2, he put me on various medications; unfortunately, none of which worked, but one actually started to cause me to display symptoms of bipolar disorder. I woke up one morning and bought a car on Craigslist on a whim. I had absolutely no business doing that. I came home after buying the car and freaked out because I had just bought a car! I punched several holes in the wall out of anger; it was completely nuts. Fortunately, I could sell the car the same day and not lose any money, so no harm and no foul, except for the holes in the wall, which I had to explain later. What I learned on that day is that some days are going to suck, and that one did. Some days "make it to midnight" is a fight to not do something stupid.

During that time, it was more than some days being intolerable. At that point, hours were intolerable. "Making it to midnight" seemed like more of a bite of life than I could take, but I did it . . . and you can too. In order to make it through the day, I had to have something more than making it to midnight to motivate me, I had to have milestones. I picked a new movie, a planned trip to the beach, or anything I could think of to stick a carrot out in the future for me to grasp. Whenever I saw a movie trailer that looked particularly good, I would make a mental note of the release date and it would be something to look forward to, not something nebulous in the future, but something concrete, not too far in the future that I could stick in my head. Pick anything, just pick something that you would regret missing.

A Boy and His Dog

One thing I would do every day is walk my dogs; that was my quiet time. My dogs were so excited about walking and exploring all the smells that had accumulated from the previous walk; it was like they were experiencing the neighborhood for the first time every time. I wanted to know how they could do that so I started to emulate them. I started to pay very close attention to every yard, every rock, every tree and flower I could see. I tried to live the walk through their eyes, tried to make their excitement contagious, and it worked. It worked because I stopped thinking about yesterday, or tomorrow, or anything other than that moment, I focused completely on the now. An unforeseen by-product of this daily exercise is that Slick was starting to enjoy those moments of relief and he was craving it more and more. Those walks gave me moments to look forward to on particularly hard days at work; I would look forward to seeing the dogs' excitement. I don't know if Slick started thinking he was a dog or what, and honestly, I didn't care. It worked, it got me through the day and that was all I could do, at that point.

Since Slick, my mammal brain, was what I was trying to heal, I spent time with my favorite mammals, my dogs. In our brains, we have something called "mirror neurons." Imagine we are walking through the forest and neither of us had seen a bear before. Suddenly a bear jumps out from behind some trees and mauls me. You see this happening, realize there is nothing you can do for me, scream, and run away. You run away unharmed. However, next time you see a bear, you panic and run away. Why? No bear attacked you. Mirror neurons are why. When you see something happen to another person, you identify with that person. A more modern example would be if you had a co-worker approach your boss and berate him for some decision he had made. That co-worker would likely be fired or at least reprimanded. You learned from watching him what the ramifications of ripping into your boss would be.

If we can learn negatives from mirror neurons, why not positives? Why can I not see the joy and happiness in my dogs and make it my own? Why can I not see children playing and point my mirror

MAKE IT TO MIDNIGHT

neurons at them and experience their joy? You can . . . and I did. Watching my dogs get excited about a walk, watching them chase squirrels and bark at cats, and just basically do "dog stuff" helped me find my happiness.

Listen to Your Mind

For me, walking my dogs was my daily ritual that I could do to turn my neocortex off and let Slick relax. I saw happiness around me in my dogs and emulated it as best I could. I forced myself to not think about things that were not in that moment. However, you may not be a dog person or may not have access to a dog. That's fine; the goal of the exercise is to get your mind off your problems. You've probably heard that phrase thousands of times in your life "get your mind off your problems," but it's true. Remember, you are spending 24-7 with a small mammal in your head, be it a small child or a small animal, and it needs time to rest, even if you do not. It needs time to just be. Whether it's a jigsaw puzzle, working in the yard, working on a car, painting, or pottery, it does not matter, as long as it is something you are *doing*. Watching TV did not work well for me because I could stare at the screen and ruminate over my problems rather than relaxing.

Listening to your mind is a hard skill to learn, as our neocortex is accustomed to overruling our limbic system. In our modern world, I do not have the luxury of letting Slick run things day to day. I must go to work; I must take care of my responsibilities to keep food on the table. When my alarm goes off at o'stupid thirty, I "force myself" to get up. Force myself? How do I *force* myself? I know I have to get up and Slick always protests, but we get up. When I get to the kitchen, I look at the doughnuts on the counter, and Slick says, "Yay, doughnuts!" but I look at our waist and say no. I get in the car to drive to work and Slick says, "Punch it!" and I look at the speed limit sign and say no. I am at the office, and my boss calls a meeting that lasts two hours, a meeting that could have been handled in two emails. After thirty minutes, Slick says, "Get up and tell him this is stupid," but I

« 133 »

sit and continue with the meeting with a fake smile. The point is that we spend so much time "forcing ourselves," which is just another way of vetoing Slick. As you would expect, that becomes the norm, and Slick becomes anxious or depressed because he is merely a passenger on this ride. By giving Slick his time to smell the roses and stretch his legs, I am treating him like an equal and giving him time to be himself. I will go for a drive or play a board game, do whatever it takes to give him time to heal.

Journal and Track Progress

We live in an amazing time; we have access to all the accumulated knowledge in human history at our fingertips. We can communicate with anyone on the planet instantaneously and effortlessly. One of the great benefits from this technology is the ability to utilize the collective resources of the internet to help us along our journey to happiness and health. One great resource that has come out of this technological explosion are apps that can help you track your mood. On the road to recovery, there will be good days and bad days. There will be good hours and bad hours, and these apps can track those hours and days. One of the great benefits of these apps is that you can see your progress over time. The way they work is fairly simple; several times a day you tell the app how you are feeling from a scale of one to ten. Over the course of time, you can track your good days and bad days, and most importantly, you can see the trend. A graph shows how you are doing. This helped me tremendously. While I was not able to see change in myself day to day, over the course of weeks, I could see the change in the graph. I needed to see victories; I needed progress. That progress becomes hope.

Music

I have been playing guitar since I was thirteen years old. I was blessed to grow up next door to an amazing musician who pushed me to be better. One thing that he and other real musicians are able to do is to convey emotion through music. It is an amazing gift I wish I possessed. If you look at any of the arts, you see the same thing. If we stop and think about it for a moment, what is art? It is an artist conveying their emotion on canvas or sculpture or on a stage or a piece of music.

There is an iconic piece of music called "O Fortuna," which I suggest you listen to with the translated lyrics, of course. It is a song that has been in countless movies. It is powerful. It has been criticized for being overused in commercials and movies because it is so powerful. It conveys such raw emotion that it is the go-to for any intense dramatic sequence. What I was not aware of, until I started researching music as a way to heal myself, is that the song was written around a thirteenth-century poem that reads a lot like Job chapter 10! The song is a lament by a man who is frustrated with life. He cries out to fate for mercy. When I read this, the song took on a whole new meaning. What did not change was that I was in awe of the music itself. What really struck me was that a man whose name has been lost to history was profoundly frustrated with life, so to deal with his frustration, he poured his emotions on paper over seven hundred years ago. Six hundred years later, in 1936, Carl Orff took the emotions of the author and set them to music. Now a hundred years after that, we hear this music and *feel* the same emotions of the man who wrote the original poem. We know that knowledge can travel through time, but if we hear that music, we learn that so can emotion.

This is very true in my life as well. If I hear any song from *Frampton Comes Alive*, I am immediately transported back to the neighborhood pool where I spent my days during summer break in the seventies. Play the song "Wish You Were Here" by Pink Floyd, and I'm back in high school. If I hear "Good night, Sweetheart" by The Overtones I am immediately transported back to closing time at Studebakers. These were great times in my life, and there are thousands of songs like that. Thousands of songs and thousands of great memories to go with them.

Music is a tool. Use it! Earlier I stated that depression had stolen my past and anxiety was taking my future. People also say that music calms the savage beast. So what if I had a tool that calmed my anxiety, my "savage beast" and brought back great memories. Well, I do. I have music. When Slick is feeling down, I know what I need to dig out to bring him out of it. Sometimes it is some good techno, sometimes it is, ironically, blues. The point is that music can, far more than words, take us back in time. If you do not believe me, and you're between the ages of thirty-five and fifty-five, try this: go to YouTube and play "Don't You Forget about Me" by Simple Minds. If you're from my generation, you cannot hear it without having some fond memory from that era. Well, at least, I cannot.

There was some happy time in the past, some movie, some song from a day out with friends that can take you back there. Depression can be a thief, but it can also be stopped, at least for a little while. The whole point of this book is to give you the tools to make it one day at a time, to "make it to midnight." If it is 8:00 PM and you're having a particularly difficult evening, look back, find a time when life was good, then find a song to take you there.

Find What Makes You Feel Good

Port Aransas, Texas, is my favorite place in the world, or as we call it, the "White Trash Riviera." When I am particularly down, Tahoe and I will drive to Port Aransas, start a fire, pitch my tent, and watch the waves. I usually spend the night down there watching the ships go in and out of the channel, wondering about the men and women on those ships. What amazing stories they must have! Trying to imagine what led them to want to work on a ship . . . were they running from something, or to something? Were they looking for a way to see the world? Or maybe they were just people who were made to be at sea. The point is, I was focusing on their stories and not mine—by focusing on them, not me.

This allows Slick and me just to "be" for a little while. It gives me a break from the day-to-day and gives Slick some time not to worry about things. Sometimes while I'm there, we talk about whatever is going on. It is a whole lot easier to deal with our baggage when we are away from all the sources of the baggage. The only problem with Port Aransas is that it is three hours away. That is not feasible for me to escape on a regular basis. No problem. There are places closer to home.

When Slick is particularly down, he does not want to do anything. He wants to sit on the couch and watch TV, or maybe, the porch. If he is anxious, he wants to do everything at once; he wants to fix the car, and clean the house, and rearrange furniture. The problem is that sometimes, those two collide. We will be at home and part of me wants to sit and do nothing but another part wants to do everything all at once. This can be an uncomfortable place. At times like this, when Slick is agitated, the last thing he wants to do is leave the house, but that is exactly what he needs. This is the part where Jim puts Tahoe and him in the car and drives to the dog park.

Slick lives in the moment, in the here and now. The moment when we are home, he is agitated by anxiety or depression or both. As I cannot change time and I cannot change his agitation in that moment, I can change where we are. I know the dog park makes all of us happy. Think of a time when you had a friend that was down, for whatever reason. Most likely if you went to them and said, "Hey, let's go do something." They would reply, "Nah, I'm not in the mood." However, if you prodded them to go, they most likely had a good time. They had to "get out of their head" for a little while. What really was happening is that their "Slick" was sitting there ruminating over what he was upset about, and when you changed the surroundings to something that he liked, things got better.

This is what I do with myself. I know what Slick likes to do. There are times when he is unhappy, when he is in a loop of depression or anxiety. The more he sits, the less he wants to move; the more anxious he is, the more anxious he becomes. My solution that works really well is to help him break that cycle.

Have an Escape Plan

What exactly does suicide accomplish? It gets you out of the situation that is causing you pain. I recently heard of a very successful doctor who took his own life. While he was a successful doctor and made a very good living, he spent money beyond his means. One day he looked at his life and realized that even if he worked until he turned ninety, he would never be able to pay off his debt. It was then that he decided to take his own life. It is easy to Monday morning quarterback a decision such as this, but it is also easy to see why he made this decision. He had built his life and his practice with the hopes of retiring and living off the fruit of his labor, and when he realized that his dream would not be a reality, he decided there was no reason to continue living.

Many people hit that point in their lives when the pain of living exceeds the fear of dying, and they choose death. I would like to propose a third alternative: escape. When I hit my low point, I saw two alternatives: keep going like I was going, which was from all indications going to be exceedingly painful for a long time, or grab my gun and end it. There is another alternative, and that is to take a sabbatical from the life that is causing you this pain. I recently read an article about a man who wanted to take his own life, but instead of using a gun, he chose drugs. He took a trip to Mexico with the intention of buying a large amount of drugs, having an intentional overdose, and peacefully dying. What happened, instead, was that when he went to acquire the drugs in Mexico, his cab driver took him to a party instead. He stayed in Mexico and had a great time. He left the life that had driven him to that point and did not look back. He was free! After a week . . . *one week* . . . he decided life was worth living; he packed his bags and went home. Imagine if that doctor had done the same thing.

My escape plan was simple; I was going to disappear somewhere in Asia, probably Thailand. Why Thailand? Why not? The point is that I gave myself a third option; instead of ending my life, I gave myself the option to change it. I could realize all the benefits of suicide and still be alive! I had this setup with my friends, as well. I told them that there may come a day when I had to disappear and if that day came they knew what to do. I had two dogs at the time and that is all I cared about, my friends said they would happily take my dogs for me.

This may seem like a pointless solution because I never put my plan into action, but this was huge for me. Depression and anxiety can get bad enough that they control every aspect of your life. From the moment you wake up to the moment you go to sleep, assuming you sleep, depression and anxiety color every decision you make. It goes back to "hugging the cactus." When Slick was trying to get me to end our life, I gave him an alternative, and that was for us to just leave it all behind and run away. Again, we never did, but just knowing that option was available to us kept the suicide option off the table. Think about that, once there was an option other than suicide I was no longer suicidal. The option to just vanish became my new go-to because the result was the same; the problems would be behind me. The great thing was, just knowing that option was available to me and now having hope kept me going. There were a few times I almost put the plan in action, but I never did . . . just knowing I could was enough.

People with suicidal ideation usually have a plan; that plan is detailed, it is almost a fantasy to many of them—well, many of us. We play it in our heads, how it would just make the pain go away. What reading the story about the man who went to Mexico taught me was that I could have a plan, I could fantasize about the plan, I could even put the plan into action, and I would still be alive to enjoy it!

Compliment People

Several years ago, I was in Colorado working on a huge IT project. I remember one morning that I was in a particularly foul mood for some reason or another. I was walking out of the hotel and down the street to the office I was working in when I saw a lady who looked very well put together. She had obviously taken a lot of time and effort to look as good as she did. Before I had time to think about it, I told her, "You look really nice." When I said this her face lit up and she gave me a very genuine "thank you for noticing, that made my day." And with that, we walked our separate ways. What I noticed about fifteen seconds later is that my foul mood had gone away. My brain had shifted from being in a foul mood, thinking about work to how I had just made someone's day. Someone I never knew and would never see again was going to have a good day because I had spoken four words.

I could not begin to tell you the mechanism behind how that works. I do know that when I do something nice for someone I feel good afterward. So let's be honest for a moment . . . does it matter what the mechanism is, if it works? Look at the world we were created in, communities were everything. People lived in communities and constantly had people around them. I remember growing up in the seventies. The routine was simple: go to school, come home, drop the backpack, and go outside and play. The adults in the neighborhood had a similar routine. They would come home from work, set down the briefcase, and go outside and sit together and talk while we played. People connected on a personal level. We, as a species, have never been more connected and lonelier at the same time. Just a small act of reaching out to a stranger and saying something complimentary can make their day and yours. "Making it to midnight" is much easier with a smile on your face.

Ceteris Paribus

When I was in college (the first time), I was an economics major. I had no great love for economics. To be honest, I couldn't have cared less about it, but I wanted a degree, and it was the degree that got me out of college the fastest. That should give you insight into the kind of man I was at twenty-three. One of the great lessons I have learned in life is that every experience, even the bad ones, can be a learning experience. One thing I took with me from that degree is the phrase "Ceteris paribus." "Ceteris paribus" is the Greek phrase for "all things remaining constant." If you look at any problem in life and want to isolate the source of the problem, the first thing you have to do is eliminate all things that are *not* the source of the problem. People tend to change things when something is bothering them. For me, I would buy guitars or cars or something like that. I think it was because there were things in my life that I was unable to change, so I decided to change the things I could.

A Tale of Two Parties

The other night, I had a party with some of my friends. We've been friends for over twenty years. They know I have sleep issues and they kept me up until 3:30 AM! I was stunned that guys my age were able to stay up so late. To add insult to injury, I bought some really good chips and salsa from a local restaurant and they ate it like it was cheap store bought stuff. When that was gone, they went into the pantry and got the store-bought stuff! None of them said thank you for it. Sure, one friend brought some frozen taquitos from Costco and some cheese and meat, but the rest of them just showed up, ate my food, drank most of my beer, and kept me up late. I have a big movie screen out in my back yard and one of them had requested a movie called *Blood of Heroes*. We watched this movie countless times when we were roommates. So I obliged and put on the movie and then half the time they were inside and not out watching it with me!

I woke up the next morning to what looked like the remains of a trailer park after a tornado. There were beer bottles and half-eaten taquitos everywhere! I went outside and it looked like the tornado had made a second appearance outside, there was crap everywhere. I can only imagine how much went over the fence. Now I'm just waiting for a note from the homeowners' association about the noise and trash. Would it have been so hard to clean up a little before they left? These people are supposed to be my friends, after all.

Take two:

The other night, I had a party with some of my friends. These guys were my roommates back in college, and they are my family. I am beyond blessed to have all of them in my life. The funniest thing about this group is that we are all so different, yet we would go to the ends of the earth for one another. We have the type of friendship that can only exist after many years and many miles. These are the guys you call at 3:00 AM after a bad breakup and they come over with beer and a sympathetic ear. And speaking of 3:00 AM, that's the time the party wrapped up! It was great to catch up with everyone, as getting us all together at the same time is damn near impossible. The reason for the party was one of the crew who lives in Japan had come for a visit, so we all needed to get together. Since he had been in Japan for so long, I bought some true South Texas chips and Salsa. One of our other friends had grabbed some taquitos from Costco because we needed some cheap college food to take us back to the good 'ole days.

There's a movie called *Blood of Heroes* that we watched countless times when we all lived together. One of my friends suggested we play it on my big movie screen in the backyard. As we sat and watched the movie, it was like we were back in 1995 again. Fortunately, we watched it so many times we all know the dialogue so none of us really paid attention to the movie, but it was a great idea to have it on. As I looked around my backyard, and then into the house, seeing all the joy and history that I was a part of, I realized how incredibly lucky I am to have these guys as my family.

I don't know how much beer was consumed, but if I had to guess, it was all of it! As I walked around the house picking up the beer bottles and half-eaten taquitos, I got to relive all the jokes and laughter all over again. I looked around my house and realized how blessed I am to have a place where everyone feels at home. Tahoe was not as happy as I was as we kept him up late, but he got over it. It took me a good hour and a half to clean up after the party, but what a blessing to be able to do that for my friends. We are adults now, we have adult problems and adult responsibilities, but for one night we were just "the guys" again.

I could have chosen to view the party through either lens, and to be honest, I have viewed these kinds of events through both. Now I choose to view my life through the lens of how blessed I am. Sometimes perception is reality.

The Mental Illness Paradox

If I had a dollar for every time someone told me "just think happy thoughts" or "you have to choose to be happy," I would not be writing this book because I would have been crushed under the weight of the dollars. Here is the paradox of mental illness; you spend all your energy pretending everything is okay. You go to work and put on the happy face, you force yourself to go out and be with people because that is what you are supposed to do; that's what society expects from you, so you do it. Every so often, though, there comes a day when the mask becomes too heavy and the façade cracks and comes crashing down; the day when you wake up and say, "I can't play the game today." The day when you want to tell the world how badly you feel, so you do. You find a friend or a family member, and you tell them how badly you feel. You completely unload the burden you've been hiding behind your smile for months or even years. Then they give you "the look." The look of confusion mixed with disbelief and dismissal. The look of "oh, it's not that big of a deal, you're fine, everyone goes through this." Sometimes you even get an eye roll and a look that says "Oh, come on, you're just being dramatic."

Shortly after you receive "the look," you will hear something like "you just need to choose to be happy," or "everyone goes through this." People will say it's not real, but it is; because depression is something that is not physically observed, people will doubt its existence, insisting that it is all in your head (because technically it is), which implies that there is something wrong with you. People tend to believe this when they compare you to themselves and if you are not like them, then the only conclusion you can draw is that you are defective. When we hear statements like "everyone goes through that," it reinforces the feeling that we already feel, which is, "there is something wrong with me."

When I experience a situation like this, I cannot help but feel ashamed. If it is true that everyone goes through this, then my complaining means that I am weak. Herein lies the paradox. Everyone has ups and downs, we all have emotions. *Not* everyone has depression. *Not* everyone has an anxiety disorder. *Not* everyone has PTSD. Those of us who do spend so much time and energy cultivating a persona that is happy and healthy are so adept at putting on the façade, that people believe us. We smile through our day and we use all of our energy to keep the lie going. We can hardly blame those we reach out to, as we have led them to believe everything is okay.

When the day comes that pretending is too much, we reach out for help, and that person looks at us with confusion and possible disappointment. I have had people I confided in say things like "Hey, I like being your friend, but I did not sign on for this, you need to go talk to someone," to which I reply, "I thought I was." When this happened to me on more than one occasion, I said to myself, "Lesson learned, I will not reach out to anyone" . . . then I met Travis Walton.

On November 5, 1975, Travis Walton and his logging crew were driving down a mountain road in Arizona. As they made their way down the winding road after a long day of logging, the driver of the truck abruptly stopped driving and pointed to something hovering over a group of trees just off the road. The object was a flying saucer. Against the protests of the other five men, Travis Walton got out of the truck to investigate. As he approached the object, a beam of light came out of the craft and knocked him to the ground. His friends, fearing he had been killed, drove away to get the police.

When they returned with the police, Travis and the UFO were gone. There was no trace of either of them. For the next five days, there was a massive search conducted by the sheriff's department. During the search, the sheriff began to suspect that the logging crew had killed Walton and disposed of the body. Five days later, just after midnight on the sixth day, Walton's brother-in-law received a phone call from Travis. He was badly dehydrated and injured. He was in a phone booth at a gas station on a mountain road. The incident was made into a movie called *Fire in the Sky*. Definitely worth watching.

Forty years after this incident happened, I met Travis Walton. Sylvia, Tahoe, and I had gone to the Roswell UFO Festival, and he was standing in front of a booth where they were selling the DVD of the movie. I walked up and introduced myself and spoke with him for a few minutes. He struck me as a man who is genuine and honorable. In forty years, his story has remained unchanged, despite countless skeptics trying to debunk and dispute his account of the events. His confidence in his testimony inspired me. Then he said something that changed my whole perspective on mental illness. He said, "To the experienced, no proof is necessary, to the skeptic, no proof is enough." This rang so true for me; someone who has experienced anxiety or depression does not need proof, and those who have not, will never understand.

Travis Walton was an inspiration to me, he boldly proclaimed that he had been abducted by aliens and was held captive aboard their ship for five days. In the face of ridicule and skepticism, Travis Walton gives all the details of his encounter and, honestly, could not have cared less who believed him or not. I decided to adopt this philosophy when I would talk to people about my anxiety and depression. I am no longer apologetic for it, I am not ashamed of it, it is just part of who I am. Depression and anxiety are *not* a sign of weakness, if anything, it is a sign of someone who has been too strong for too long. Mental illness is not something to be ashamed of or to apologize for; it is part of who we are.

Now, when I tell someone about how Slick and I are not getting along, I approach the situation differently. The first thing I say is, "I do not need you to fix this, I just need you to listen." Most people, after hearing their friend has a problem, react by trying to offer a solution. This is great if you are talking about finding a mechanic or being frustrated with the season finale of a TV show, but mental illness is different. Every time I had a friend say, "Well, what you need to do is . . ." I would stop them and say, "I just need you to listen." My closest friends understand. They have the attitude of "I do not understand what you are going through, but whatever you need, I am here."

We all arrived at this place in our lives by different routes. Some of it is nature and some nurture. Now what I tell my friends is that I just need to vent. I need them to care. I need a safe place to land. Your friends and family genuinely want to help you, but they do not know how. So tell them. Tell them you appreciate their trying to help, but you need validation not advice. The best thing I can hear when I am having one of those days is "Wow, Jim, that sucks."

Event Horizon

In astrophysics, there is a phenomenon call an event horizon. When a star runs out of fuel to burn, all the mass of that star collapses in on itself and a black hole is formed. When this happens, the gravity from it pulls in any object that gets caught in its gravitational field and that object becomes part of the black hole. The gravity generated from a black hole is so intense that nothing can escape from it. As an object gets pulled into the black hole, its velocity increases until it approaches the speed of light. The event horizon is the region of space surrounding the black hole from which nothing, not even light, can escape. Think of it kind of like a whirlpool. If you are swimming in the ocean and a whirlpool forms, you may be able to swim away from it if you are at a safe distance. However, there is a point at which the strength of the whirlpool will exceed your ability to swim and you will be sucked in.

Something similar happens when I drive by an electronics store. When I am feeling down and want some "retail therapy" to make me feel better, I must be mindful of my surroundings. There is a point around that store that if I get too close my car will magically drive itself into the parking lot, and I will leave with some electronics trinket that I do not need. The same thing works with addicts and people with depression. When we feel badly, regardless of whether it is from an addiction or from depression, we want that bad feeling to stop. Unfortunately, the thing that makes us feel better is damaging to us in the long run.

There is an electronics store that I drive by when I go home from work. It is a geek's paradise. On days when I have struggled, Slick will tell me when we get in the car, "Hey, let's swing by the toy store and see what new stuff they have." I know as soon as I think this, I need to take an alternate route home. I know that if I drive home on my normal route, I will see the store and Slick will compel me to turn in. This is what I counsel my clients who struggle with alcohol to do. When they have a bad day, and feel they need a drink, find a route home that does not take them by their regular bar.

People Calories

I messaged a friend of mine once on Facebook and she replied, "Sorry, Jim, I've burned all my people calories today, I'll message you tomorrow." I suppose I should have been insulted, but it was pretty funny so I let it slide. She did message me the next day. What she said got me thinking though . . . people calories. One of the mistakes I made when I was going through depression was trying to pretend I was fine. Part of that act meant being available as a counselor to friends of mine in need.

Imagine one day you woke up and looked in the mirror and said to yourself, "Wow, I need to lose a few." Okay, I don't have to imagine it. Upon this revelation that you need to lose weight you decide to go to a diet retreat. At the retreat, your diet is strictly monitored, your food is measured and you receive five hundred calories at breakfast, five hundred at lunch, and five hundred at dinner. The following morning at breakfast, you get two eggs and two pieces of toast. A man next to you asks for a piece of toast because he is really struggling. You see he is in distress so you give him a piece of your toast. At lunch, you sit next to him again. He asks how you are doing and you reply, "I'm okay, I'm a little hungrier than I expected to be." Realizing that he had eaten your second piece of toast that morning, he offers you part of his lunch. You thank him and happily take the extra food.

That night at dinner, they serve beef and asparagus. You really like asparagus so you ask a lady next to you if you can have her asparagus. She replies "Of course, I'm not terribly hungry tonight anyway. I'm in a good place, I'm happy to help you out." You are happy you got the extra asparagus and she feels good for helping you. Life is good.

You are unaware of it but next to you another lady saw the transaction. She leans over and asks you for a piece of your steak, she reminds you that you have more than you need, and she is really hungry. You cut her off a small portion and continue dinner. The following morning, she sits next to you again. As you are eating your breakfast, she complains about how small the portions are. She apologetically asks you for a piece of toast. You think to yourself, "Well, I'm not *that* hungry" and give it to her. Lunch comes around and so does she. She says, "I'm so sorry to bother you again, I guess I have a fast metabolism, can I have some of your lunch? I'll pay you back at dinner, I promise." You begrudgingly give her some of your sandwich and continue eating and talking with the other guests.

Dinner comes and you sit at the table, and your new friend sits across from you. You ask her politely for some of her asparagus. She replies, "They did not give me very much and this has to last me until morning, I'm sorry I cannot spare any." She eats her dinner and enjoys the conversation with the other guests. You, however, are a little perturbed; however you do not want to confront her because, come on, it's not that big of a deal, right? It's just asparagus. Plus, you do not want to cause a scene. You decide to be the (metaphorically) bigger person and let it go.

Breakfast comes and like clockwork so does she. She tells you that her dinner did not fill her up and she is terribly hungry. She asks again for a piece of your toast. Now ask yourself . . . do you give it to her? Do you forget how she slighted you last night? Do you tell her no, because you had always been there for her, but when you needed her, she would not repay the favor? Just like she took your nutritional calories, she also took your people calories . . . without hesitation and without remorse.

The average human burns roughly two thousand calories per day. Extroverts are people who replenish their people calories by being around other people while introverts are refueled by being alone. I think I am a little of both. There are people in my circle of friends and acquaintances who replenish my people calories. They are people that I am always happy to see. People who I feel better after I see them than I did before. Conversation is easy, their caring and interest in my wellbeing is genuine, as mine is for them. They are friends; they are people I can call if I need help and they can call me. We have a symbiotic relationship.

However, there are people (or were) who I would only hear from when they needed something. What I realized is that these people, like the lady in the story, needed more people calories than I did, so they would take mine. This was fine when I was healthy and had calories to spare, but when my life took a negative turn, I no longer had the energy (calories are fuel) to help them. They always seemed to have a crisis. They needed to move suddenly, or borrow money, or they had yet another romantic interest lie to them. They always had drama and they wanted me to fix it or at least be a sympathetic ear. This is something I am happy to do when I am able, but for several years, I was not able . . . yet I continued to do it. I continued to help, I continued to listen.

Then one day, something clicked. I have a block feature on my phone. Without warning or explanation, I blocked two of them . . . and it felt good. It felt like I had told the lady at the retreat "No, you cannot have my toast, go talk to the people running the camp. Go fix your own problem." After a week, I unblocked them. A couple of hours later one of them texted me and said "Hey, are you okay?" I replied, "I'm great, I just ran out of people calories." She immediately replied, "Oh, good, I need your help." Blocked.

After some time had passed, I unblocked her and explained that I am happy to be her friend. I am happy to go get a drink or chat, but I cannot be her savior. I cannot be the person she calls when she needs help because I am not in a position to give her any help. I have problems of my own, and while I can handle what has been handed me, I cannot handle any more than that. She was mad for a little while, but she got over it. Now when she calls, she asks, "Hey, how are you doing?" And I believe she really is interested in how I am. The lesson I learned is that you have to teach people how to treat you. If every time they call they take your people calories, maybe you need to reevaluate that relationship. I was fortunate, I blocked five people over the next few weeks, and all of them are still my friends, we just re-negotiated the terms of our relationship.

When I had this epiphany, I went back to the friend I originally messaged and asked her if I was draining her people calories. She replied, "Yea, sometimes." I corrected that as well.

David Had the Stones

Numbers chapter 16 tells the story of a rebellion against Moses. A man named Korah decided he was not happy with the way Moses was running things so he wanted to be in charge. He and his followers were angry with Moses for leading them out of Egypt, the land flowing with milk and honey (where they were slaves) and into the wilderness. In verse 4, Moses tells Korah, "In the morning the Lord will show who belongs to him and who is holy, and he will have that person come near him. The man he chooses he will cause to come near him." The next morning came, "And the earth opened its mouth and swallowed them and their households, and all those associated with Korah, together with their possessions. They went down alive into the realm of the dead, with everything they owned; the earth closed over them, and they perished and were gone from the community." This story is a great example of what God can do if he chooses. Korah and his followers chose to defy God and his chosen emissary Moses at their own peril.

I always recall this story whenever I hear someone invoke the story of David and Goliath. When people talk about David and Goliath, they do so in the context that the "little guy," David fought a giant, Goliath. The name Goliath has become synonymous with the idea of something that is almost insurmountable. Whenever a small company is going up against a larger company it is referred to as a "David and Goliath" story. The same thing occurs when someone decides to fight city hall, it's David vs. Goliath. I've read the story . . . David won. To be honest, it always makes me chuckle. The story of David and Goliath was not about a small shepherd fighting against a giant warrior . . . the story of David and Goliath was a story about a man, Goliath, picking a fight with God. Of course, Goliath was going to lose. It was not a matter of if God was going to defeat Goliath, it was a matter of how. Rather than swallow up Goliath and the Philistines in the earth like He did with Korah, God chose to send David.

If you read the story of David and Goliath in 1 Samuel 17, you will notice two things. First, David's own people and even his own brother do not believe he is capable of defeating Goliath. They almost see the idea as comical. According to verse 28, "When Eliab, David's oldest brother, heard him speaking with the men, he burned with anger at him and asked, 'Why have you come down here? And with whom did you leave those few sheep in the wilderness?' I know how conceited you are and how wicked your heart is; you came down only to watch the battle." Eliab sees David as just a shepherd boy and believes he has nothing to offer to the army. However, David had been preparing for this battle his whole life; he just did not know it until that day. Like the boy in John 6:9 who gave Jesus the fish and bread, God had been preparing David for this moment. Eliab also accuses David of being conceited and wicked; however, what David says in response shows he is neither conceited or wicked, he is confident in the Lord.

The second thing you notice is that David agrees that he is not capable of defeating Goliath . . . but God is. When the conversation between David and the soldiers was reported to Saul, he sent for David. David convinced him that he could defeat Goliath. David said, "Your servant has been keeping his father's sheep. When a lion or a bear came and carried off a sheep from the flock, I went after it, struck it and rescued the sheep from its mouth. When it turned on me, I seized it by its hair, struck it and killed it. Your servant has killed both the lion and the bear; this uncircumcised Philistine will be like one of them, because he has defied the armies of the living God. The Lord who rescued me from the paw of the lion and the paw of the bear will rescue me from the hand of this Philistine." David said "The Lord who rescued me from the paw of the lion and bear . . ." He gives full credit to God and has full confidence that God will deliver him again.

Both depression and anxiety are represented in this story. Eliab represents our depression. He is that voice that has known us our entire lives; he knows our weaknesses and insecurities. When we decide we are going to march on the battlefield and take on our Goliath, Eliab is there to tell us all the reasons we cannot defeat him. Goliath represents our anxiety. Goliath stands in our path toward our promised land. He is a giant that taunts us and insults us and above all tries to intimidate us into not challenging him. People with anxiety and depression are like David. Standing alone in a desert, listening to taunts from the past and future, hearing a chorus of reasons we cannot go on. Eliab and Goliath are that voice in our heads that will not be silenced. It is the voice that says, "You are not strong enough to get that job."

"You are not as successful as your friends, you're a failure." "She is too pretty for you." "He is out of your league." They say that and any of a thousand other things to keep us from coming onto the battlefield and facing our Goliath.

When King Saul finally relents and accepts David as his champion in 1 Samuel 17, he tries to fit David with his armor. "After trying it on, David said, "I cannot go in these," he said to Saul, "because I am not used to them." So he took them off. Then he took his staff in his hand, chose five smooth stones from the stream, put them in the pouch of his shepherd's bag, and with his sling in his hand, approached the Philistine." Rather than put on the armor of the King, David put on the full armor of God as described in Ephesians 6. "Finally, be strong in the Lord and in his mighty power. Put on the full armor of God, so that you can take your stand against the devil's schemes. For our struggle is not against flesh and blood, but against the rulers, against the authorities, against the powers of this dark world and against the spiritual forces of evil in the heavenly realms. Therefore, put on the full armor of God, so that when the day of evil comes, you may be able to stand your ground, and after you have done everything, to stand."

The only difference between David and the rest of the army of Israel is that David had the stones to step on the battlefield, he stepped out there with the confidence that God was with him. David only had to defeat Goliath once; we have to defeat him every day. Like Sisyphus rolling the stone up the hill every day, we have a constant battle. However, unlike Sisyphus, who was being punished by the gods, our God is there to roll the stone with us. I can tell you from personal experience, every day you roll that stone up the hill, the stone gets a little smaller. Then one day you realize that it is so small that you can put it in your pouch and go slay Goliath with it. Vaya con Dios . . . Go with God.

JIM DENNING IS a licensed professional counselor and pastor living in San Antonio. He holds master of arts degrees in counseling and ministry. He was formerly a senior information technology professional, member of Mensa, and a technical trainer at the NASA Jet Propulsion Laboratory. However, his greatest education in human behavior came from his years spent as a bartender and prison minister. Jim did not know it at the time, but all his education and experience that he sought to use to help others actually ended up saving his life.

In 2009, Jim was diagnosed with bipolar disorder II, major depression, generalized anxiety disorder, malaise, ADHD, and suicidal ideation. He was denied life insurance and was told to go on disability because his doctors labeled his symptoms as "treatment resistant."

Unwilling to accept this prognosis, Jim turned to God and his education and experience to develop a set of tools and protocols to combat his situation. Today he is medication free and happier than he has ever been. It was all about changing the way he viewed his brain and himself.